AF252015

The Twelve Tribes

a meditation on art, prophecy, and poetry

Yonnah Ben Levy & Chaim Bezalel

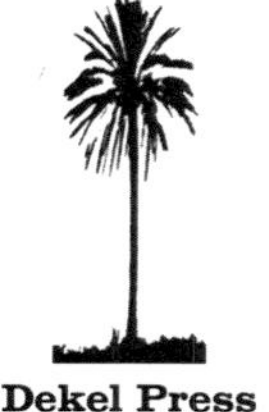

Dekel Press

ISBN: 978-0-9995958-3-1
Library of Congress: 2017963452

FIRST EDITION

Dedicated to our Rabbis and teachers: Cantor Sidney Rosenfeld ז״ל, Rabbi Matthew Futterman, Alan Zeffren, Rabbi and Scribe Gustavo Surazski, Barbara Greenberg, and Rabbi Anita Steiner

© 2018 by Yonnah Ben Levy and Chaim Bezalel
All rights reserved
Printed in the United States of America

Published by Dekel Press   www.dekelpress.com

Introduction

This book contains words and pictures relating to two different but related art projects, "Bowls of Blessing" (2011) and "Urim and Thummim" (1991). Both are based on our endeavor to understand two cryptic portions of the Bible: Jacob's "blessings" over his twelve sons and the urim and thummim, the oracular elements related to the breastplate of the High Priest with its twelve inlaid stones symbolizing the twelve tribes. In the twenty years between the two projects, the questions became more important than the answers.

The Bible is in the public domain, at least certain versions of it including the original versions, the Greek Septuagint which is the earliest translation, and the the King James Bible. Some translations are under copyright. The translations given in this book are from non-copyrighted versions or sometimes, for the sake of clarity or contrast, I will give a literal word for word translation from the Hebrew, which is often quite pithy.

Just as translations vary, so do interpretations. Many of the quotations are poetry or prophecy, which was often the same thing. Both were declamations, at a time when words and oaths held great power. As we all know, poetry is licensed to use many techniques such as metaphor, hyperbole, and sometimes even deliberate obfuscation. To explain poetry in plain language, especially poetry in translation, is like trying to explain a joke. As the exasperated humorist would say, "You had to be there."

The subject of the twelve tribes of Israel has long been a mystery. Ten of them have been lost for 2700 years. The northern tribes broke away from the short lived unification with Judah to form their own kingdom of Israel which was conquered by the Assyrians two hundred years later. They were then scattered throughout the empire.

There have been many theories put forward over the centuries. Some believed that they were removed to a land beyond the mythical river, Sambatyon, so treacherous that it carried boulders in its swift current, which abated only on the Sabbath when it was forbidden to travel. The 19th century brought forth new theories. Some believed, and still do, that the Indians in America are the lost tribes or that the British are. Some, including some anthropologists, believe that the Pashtun Tribe, including the Taliban, are descended from the lost tribes of Israel.

What we have learned in the twenty years between these two bodies of work is to withhold judgment, because prophecies often are difficult to understand and even more difficult to time. The very name, Israel, can mean different things. It can refer to that short-lived united kingdom under David and Solomon, or to the northern tribes after their secession. It can be applied to the adherents of the Jewish religion, which is not simply a religion but also a nation that maintained its identity in exile because of its memory of national solidarity, as well as conflict and discrimination. It can refer to the modern state of Israel. In the Bible, it can also be the name that was substituted for, or added to, the name of Jacob, which itself is often employed as a synecdoche, the poetic device in which a part is named to represent the whole.

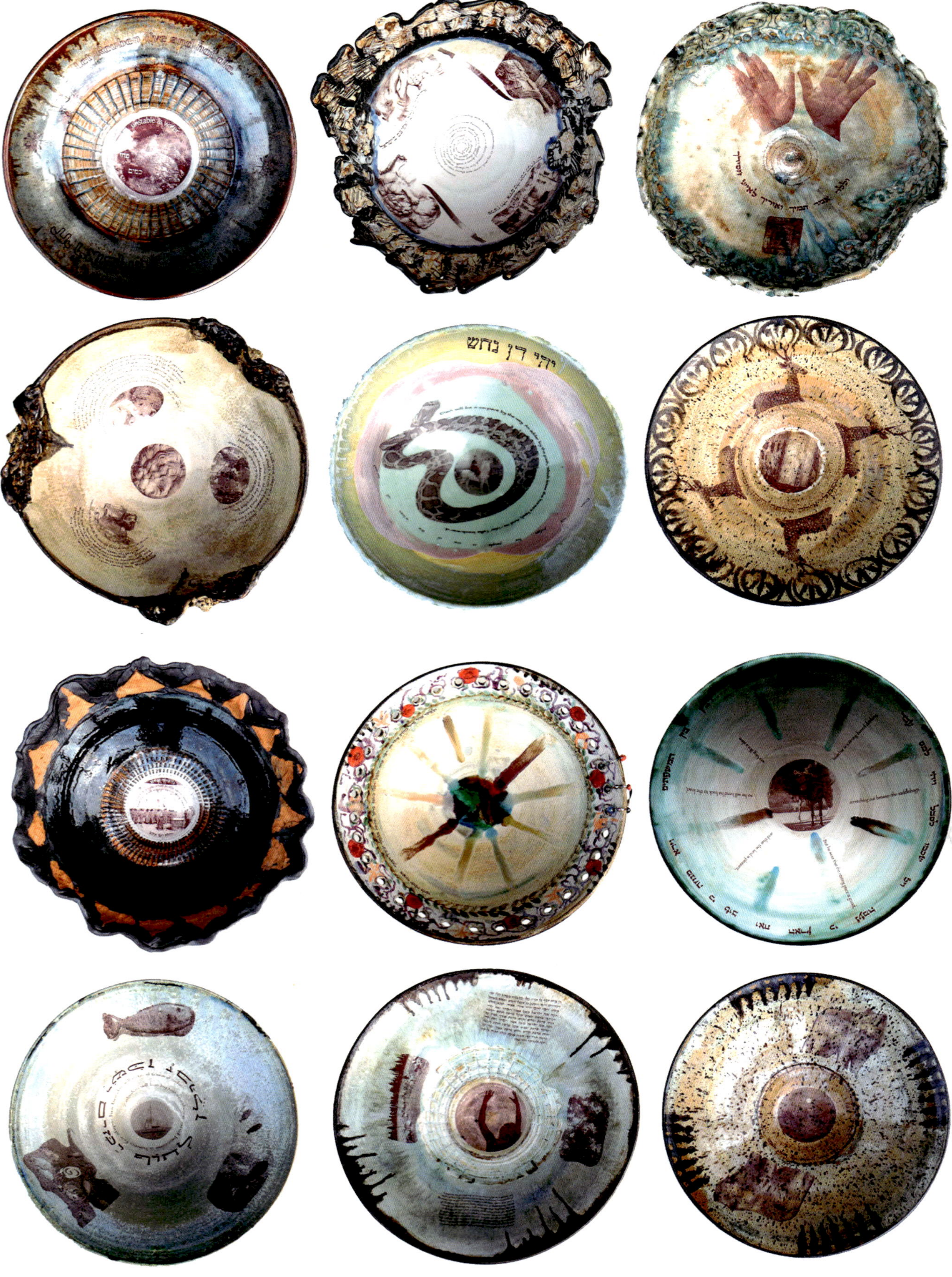

Bowls of Blessing

This series consists of twelve ceramic bowls containing both images and words that have been embedded into the glaze. The bowls illuminate, through original photographs and text in English and Hebrew, excerpts from Genesis 49, which consists of Jacob's blessings over his twelve sons, the progenitors of the twelve tribes of Israel. These sayings are poetic and are therefore are considered to have been first passed down through oral tradition making them one of the oldest parts of the Bible. They are replete with references to various animals and crops, and sometimes reference preceding events in which these sons played a role, and not always a noble one.

We have been collaborating, both in Israel, where we met and married, and in the United States for twenty-eight years, usually on paintings. Yonnah, who is also a ceramic artist and teacher, was challenged throw large bowls from an entire 25 pound sack of clay. After producing one such "perfect" bowl, the Levi bowl, one of her students accidentally knocked it onto the floor while still damp. Yonnah then hand-built the top of the bowl, and this influenced some subsequent pieces. Chaim then illuminated the bowls with original photography as well as text which were fired into the glaze. For both artists, each bowl became a meditation.

One of the antecedents for this project, particularly for the spiral script written inside each bowl, is the "Incantation Bowl" of ancient Babylon. "During the Sassanian period (224 CE – 651 CE) there were many Jewish settlers living in Babylonia in southern Iraq. They left behind many magic bowls inscribed in Aramaic with magic texts designed to protect one's wife, children, house or other property. Some of these bowls contain blessings and others curses. However, the practice of inscribing words and images in clay dates to the invention of writing itself. Many of the first narratives were written in clay.

We decided on the title "Bowls of Blessing" because they contain what has come to be known as Jacob's blessings over his sons, though they are not all positive sayings. In oracular language and poetry, in fact in all utterances stemming from oral tradition, words seem to carry more weight; before they passed from clay to parchment to paper to the ether of the computer screen. One example of the immutability of words is the story of Jacob's use of guile to steal the blessing from his elder twin brother, Esau. Isaac could not reverse his blessing, even though it was obtained through deceit.

The portion of the Bible containing these blessings is chanted in an annual cycle of Torah readings in the synagogue. The particular portion into which it falls is called "Vayechi," meaning "and he lived." These are the opening words of the portion describing Jacob's sojourn in Egypt culminating in his last words uttered over his sons. Chaim composed a twelve minute piece, "Vayechi Suite," combining the traditional chanting of this portion of the Torah with an electronic jazz accompaniment.

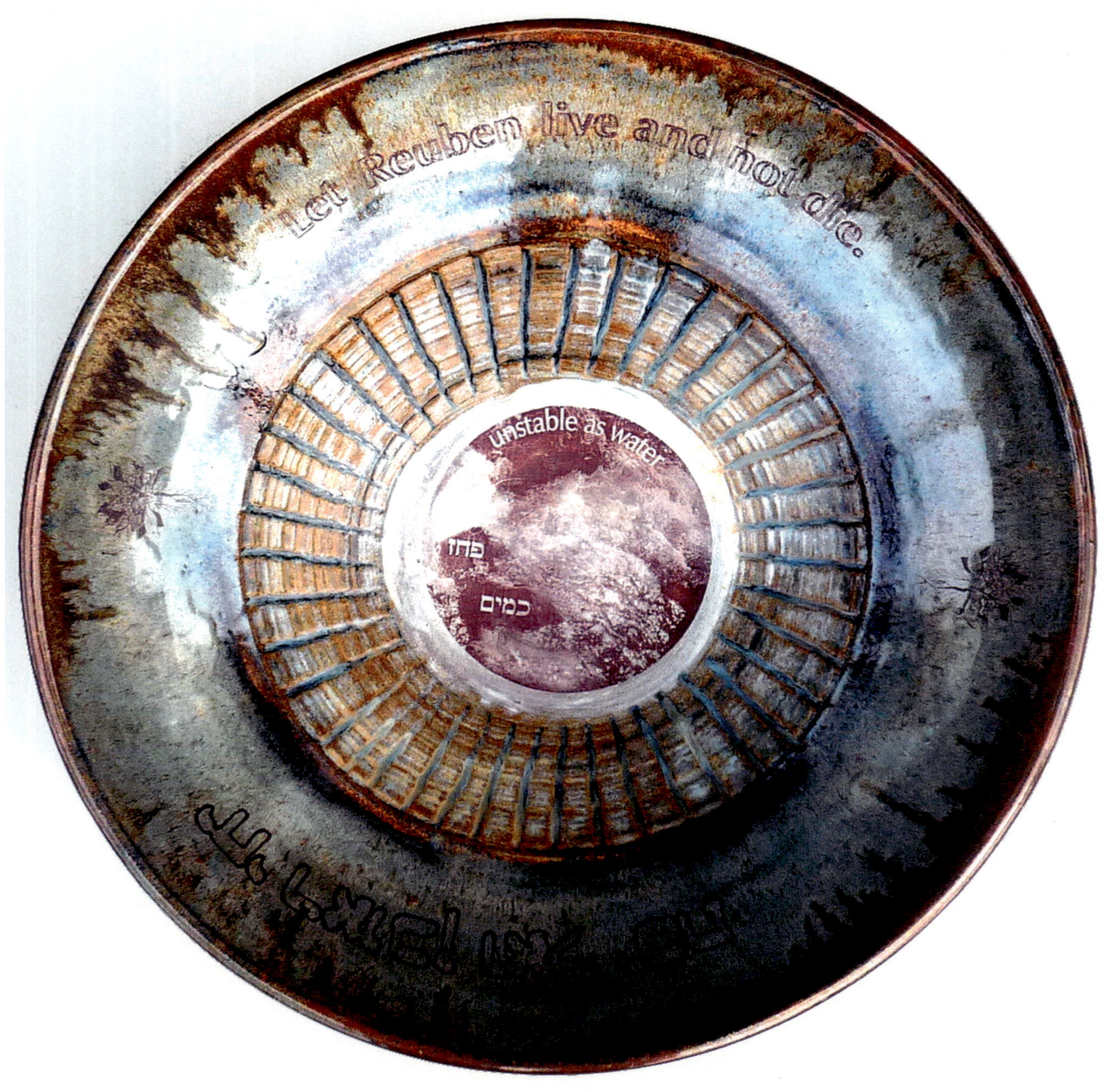

Reuben (16 in. width x 5 in. height)

"Let Reuben live and not die" (Deuteronomy 33:6) is from Moses' blessings over the twelve tribes of Israel. *"Unstable as water" is* from Jacob's prophecy over Reuben, He recounts Reuben's sexual encounter with Jacob's concubine, Bilhah, *"defiling his father's bed."* The design element in the center is turbulent water, and on the sides of the bowl are shown two mandrakes, a plant traditionally used as a symbol for the tribe of Reuben. In early peoples, the mandrake was associated with the belief that it promoted fertility and conception in barren women. Genesis 30:14 recounts the story of how Rachel bartered with her sister, Leah, a night in Jacob's bed in return for the mandrakes that Leah's son Reuben found. In addition to Leah and Rachel, Jacob produced offspring with their two handmaids, Bilhah and Zilpah.

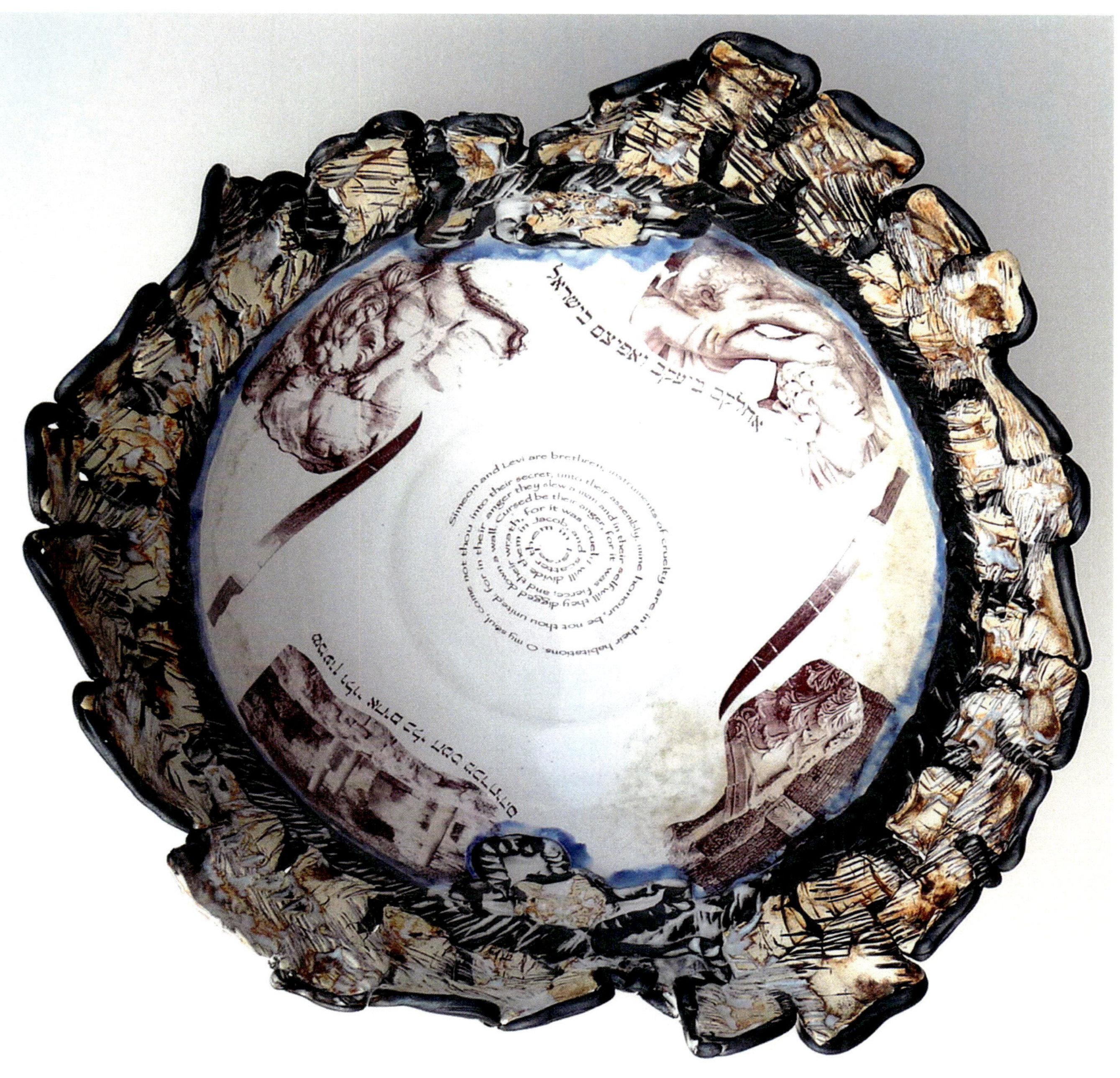

Simeon (17 in. width x 9 in. height)

"Simeon and Levi are brethren; instruments of cruelty are in their habitations. O my soul, come not thou into their secret; unto their assembly, mine honour, be not thou united: for in their anger they slew a man, and in their self will they digged down a wall. Cursed be their anger, for it was fierce; and their wrath, for it was cruel: I will divide them in Jacob, and scatter them in Israel." – Genesis 49:5-7

Jacob is referring here to the incident described in Genesis 33. Returning to the land of his birth, after a reunion with his brother Esau, Jacob pitched his tent at Shechem (present day Nablus). His only daughter, Dinah, "went out to see the daughters of the land." When the eponymous Shechem, the son of Hamor, the prince of the land saw her he "took her, and lay with her, and humiliated her." But then he fell in love with her and asked his father, Hamor (which means donkey in Hebrew) to get her for him as a wife.

Upon learning of the rape of Dinah Jacob's sons were, of course, angry. When Hamor approached them suggesting a treaty sealed by intermarriages, "the sons of Jacob answered Shechem and Hamor his father with guile … because he had defiled Dinah their sister." They insisted that all of the men of the city be circumcised. Then, after three days, when they were recuperating, Simeon and Levi went into the city, slaughtered every male including Hamor and Shechem, took Dinah out of Shechem's house, "took their flocks and their herds and their asses, and that which was in the city and that which was in the field; and all their wealth, and all their little ones and their wives, they took captive and spoiled, even all that was in the house." (It is unclear whether the house, the women, or both were despoiled. However the word that is used is related more to plunder.) Then Jacob complained, not to all of the sons who had acted in guile, but only to Simeon and Levi, who had carried out the plan. His only stated objection was that they had given him a bad name among the inhabitants of the land who far outnumbered them and could destroy them. He carried this resentment to his deathbed.

Years later, when Jacob sent all of his sons, except Benjamin, down to Egypt to purchase grain, Joseph, who had become vizier, put his brothers to the test by having Simeon bound and kept behind as a hostage until the brothers produced Benjamin. Nevertheless, Jacob refused to allow his youngest son to travel, consigning Simeon to the same fate as Joseph. "Joseph is no more and Simeon is no more." Only after the grain ran out did he allow Benjamin to accompany his brothers and redeem Simeon.

In Moses' blessings over the tribes, Simeon is the only tribe not mentioned. This has been noted by commentators, both Jewish and Christian. In the Alexandrian copy of the Septuagint (the oldest version of the Greek Septuagint, which was the first translation of the Hebrew Bible), Simeon's name was actually inserted and attached to the conclusion of the preceding prophecy relating to his older brother, Reuben, just before the verse, "Let not his men be few." However, in the original Hebrew Simeon is not mentioned. One can understand why the date of the completion of the Septuagint, Tevet 8 on the Jewish calendar, which falls in late December or early January, was declared a fast day in the Talmud. It has since been consolidated with the fast of Tevet 10, when Nebuchadnezzar II's armies besieged Jerusalem.

Personally, however, as a native English speaker, I value translations, though applying the Hebrew caveat, *kavdehu v'hoshdehu*, respect it and suspect it. As it turned out, the tribe was indeed few in number. The first census, taken after the Exodus from Egypt, counted 59,300 men. Forty years later, before entering Canaan, the number had decreased to 22,200. Ultimately the territory of Simeon was surrounded by Judah and became subsumed.

The traditional symbols of this tribe include a sword and often a wall or gate. The image of a lion goring an ox on the bowl is from an ancient marble sarcophagus found in the city of Ashkelon, Israel. "They gored an ox" is an alternative translation to "they digged down a wall," and is found in some versions of the Bible. The Hebrew text under the image of two men fighting, also from the same sarcophagus, reads: "I will divide them in Jacob, and scatter them is Israel." This is an example of the Biblical Hebrew poetic device of parallelism. The other two images inside the bowl are of columns and the base of a Corinthian column, both from among the ruins of Ashkelon. The interior walls of the bowl signify a broken wall. The exterior walls contain design elements from the Corinthian column base impressed into the clay and also a repetitive image of a sealed gate.

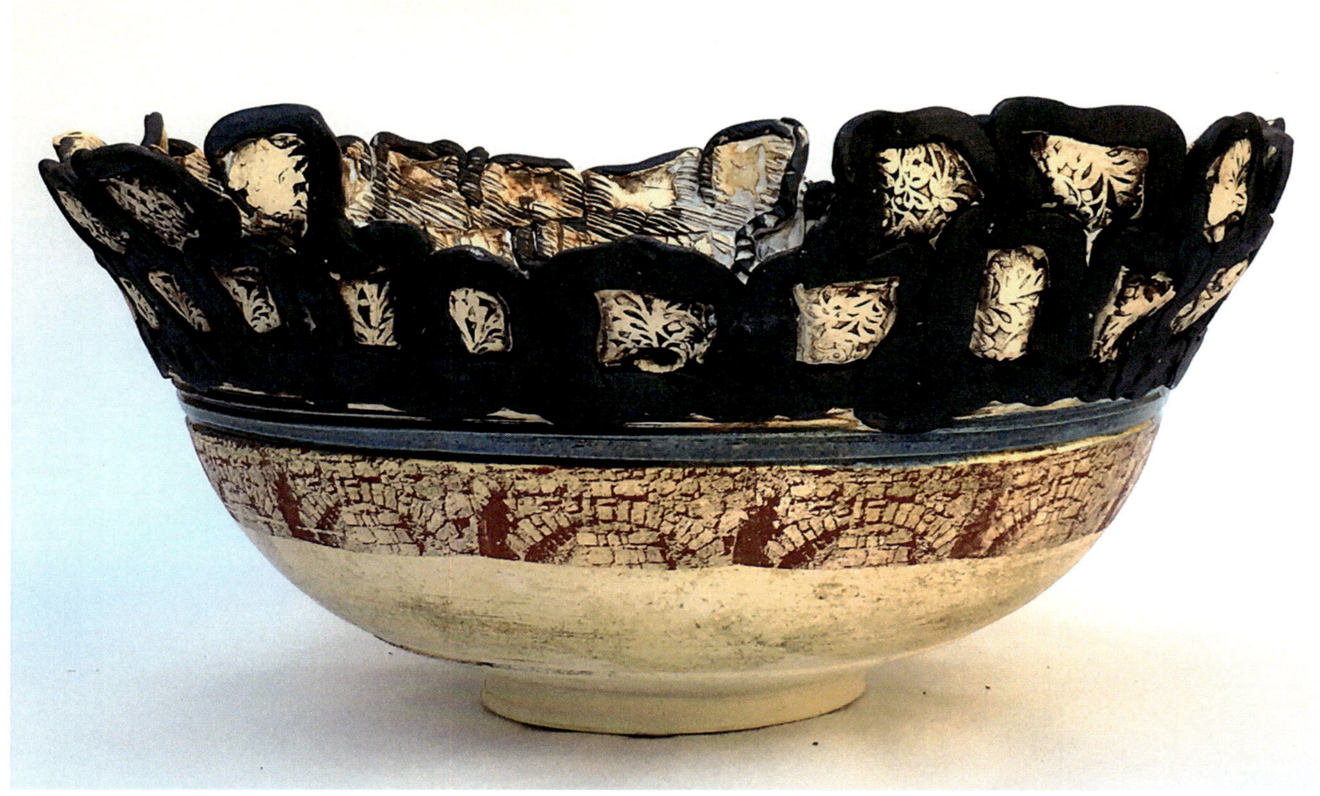

Simeon (exterior)

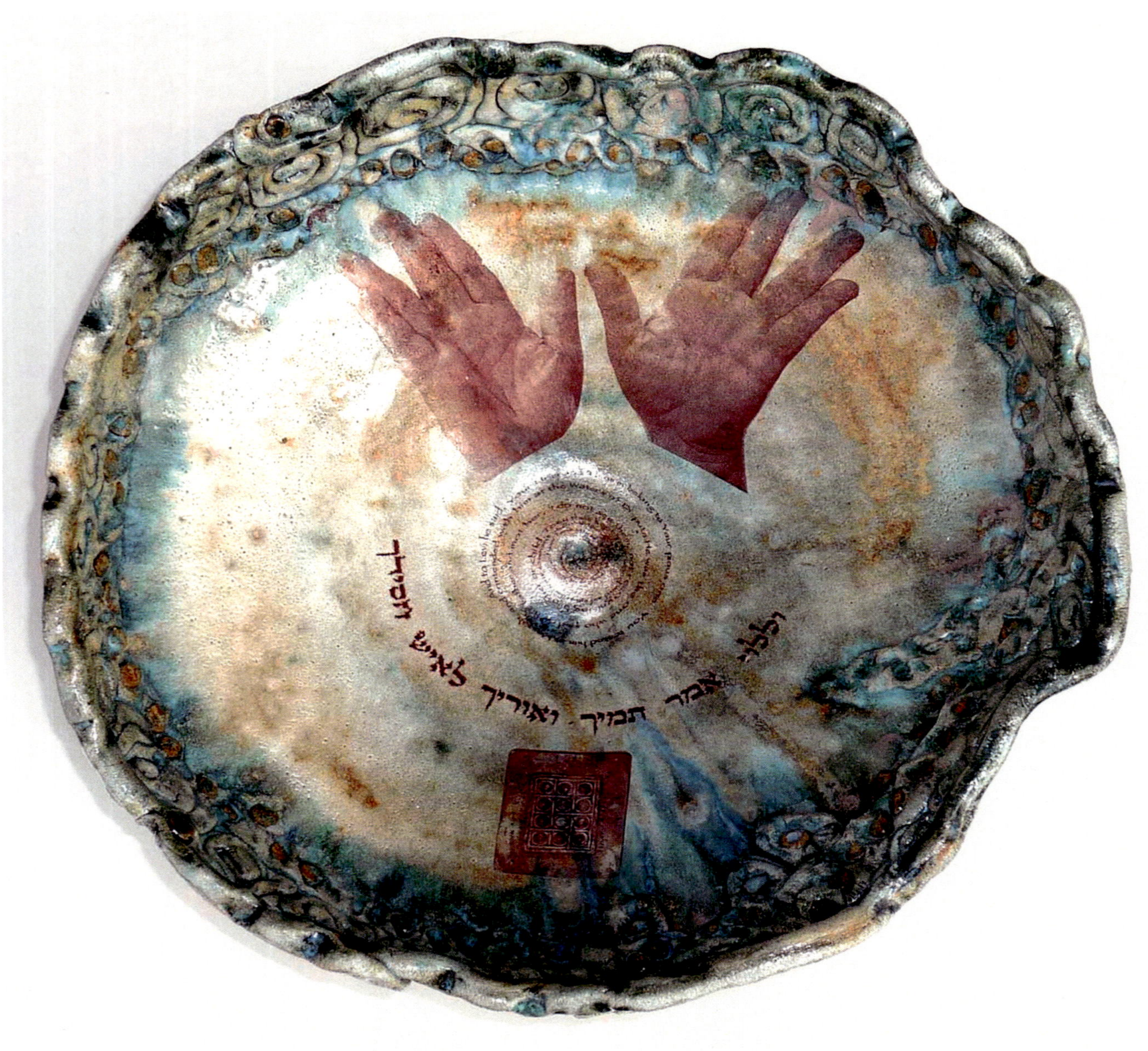

Levi (18 in. width x 7 in. height)

"And of Levi he said, Let thy Thummim and thy Urim be with thy pious one, whom thou didst prove at Massah, and with whom thou didst strive at the waters of Meribah. Who said unto his father and to his mother, I have not seen him; neither did he acknowledge his brethren, nor knew his own children: for they have observed thy word, and kept thy covenant. They shall teach Jacob thy judgments, and Israel thy law: they shall put incense before thee, and whole burnt sacrifice upon thine altar. Bless, LORD, his substance, and accept the work of his hands; smite through the loins of them that rise against him, and of them that hate him, that they rise not again." – Genesis 33:8-11

The long passage regarding Levi is not from Genesis, wherein Jacob uttered his harsh pronouncement over both Simeon and Levi. It is from Moses' blessings over the tribes. Apparently, the tribe of Levi maintained the same spirit of zealotry that their progenitor had exhibited in the massacre which took place at Shechem. When the sword was wielded once more against brothers, companions, and neighbors who had bowed down to the golden calf, the tribe of Levi was redeemed in the eyes of Moses, who had ordered the mass execution. (Exodus:32).

On the bowl, Moses' entire blessing over the tribe of Levi appears in a spiral, the text diminishing in size as it reaches the center. The Hebrew writing on the bowl is the first line of the passage and is written in scribal calligraphy. The hands are raised in the traditional gesture that the kohenim or priests, a segment of the tribe of Levi, still maintain to recite the priestly benediction (Numbers 6:24-26) over the congregation. The plaque shown below the Hebrew text is a representation of the breastplate of the High Priest, which is associated with the Urim and Thummim (further discussed in another section of this book). It contained twelve precious and semi-precious stones in their settings, representing the twelve tribes.

During the making of this bowl, Yonnah had left it to dry on the potter's wheel. It was her most perfect so far, from a 25 pound sack of clay. One of her students accidentally brushed against it knocking it to the floor. Instead of getting angry or sad, she picked it off the floor and remade it, turning it into an hand-built bowl. This influenced some of the subsequent bowls which are half wheel thrown and half hand-built. Just as the potter in the Book of Jeremiah remade a marred vessel "as it seemed good to the potter to make," it can be taken as an illustration of God's omnipotence, as well as artistic license, or redemption in spite of circumstances or imperfection. In both Biblical and modern Hebrew, the verb "to create" is only applied to God. Human beings "fashion."

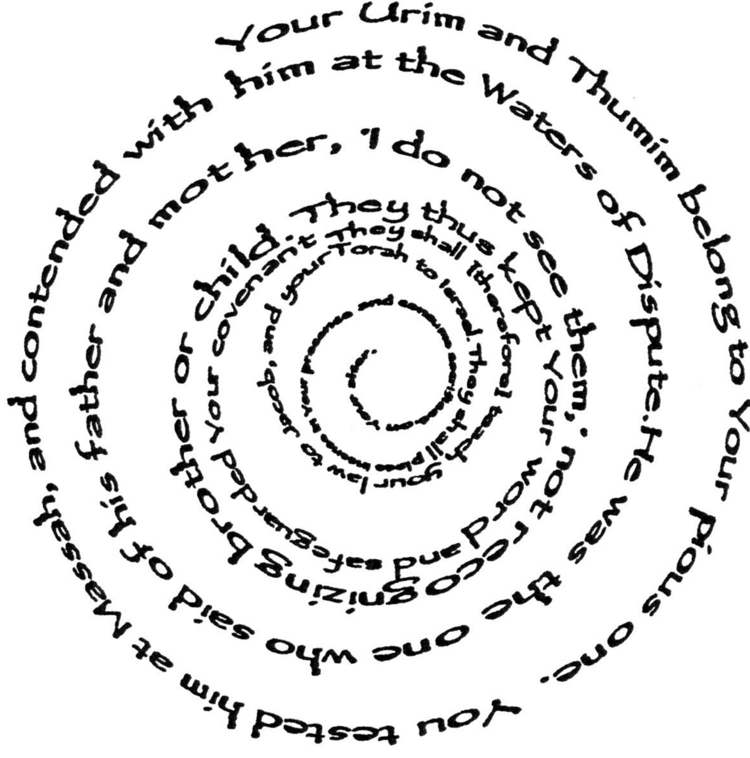

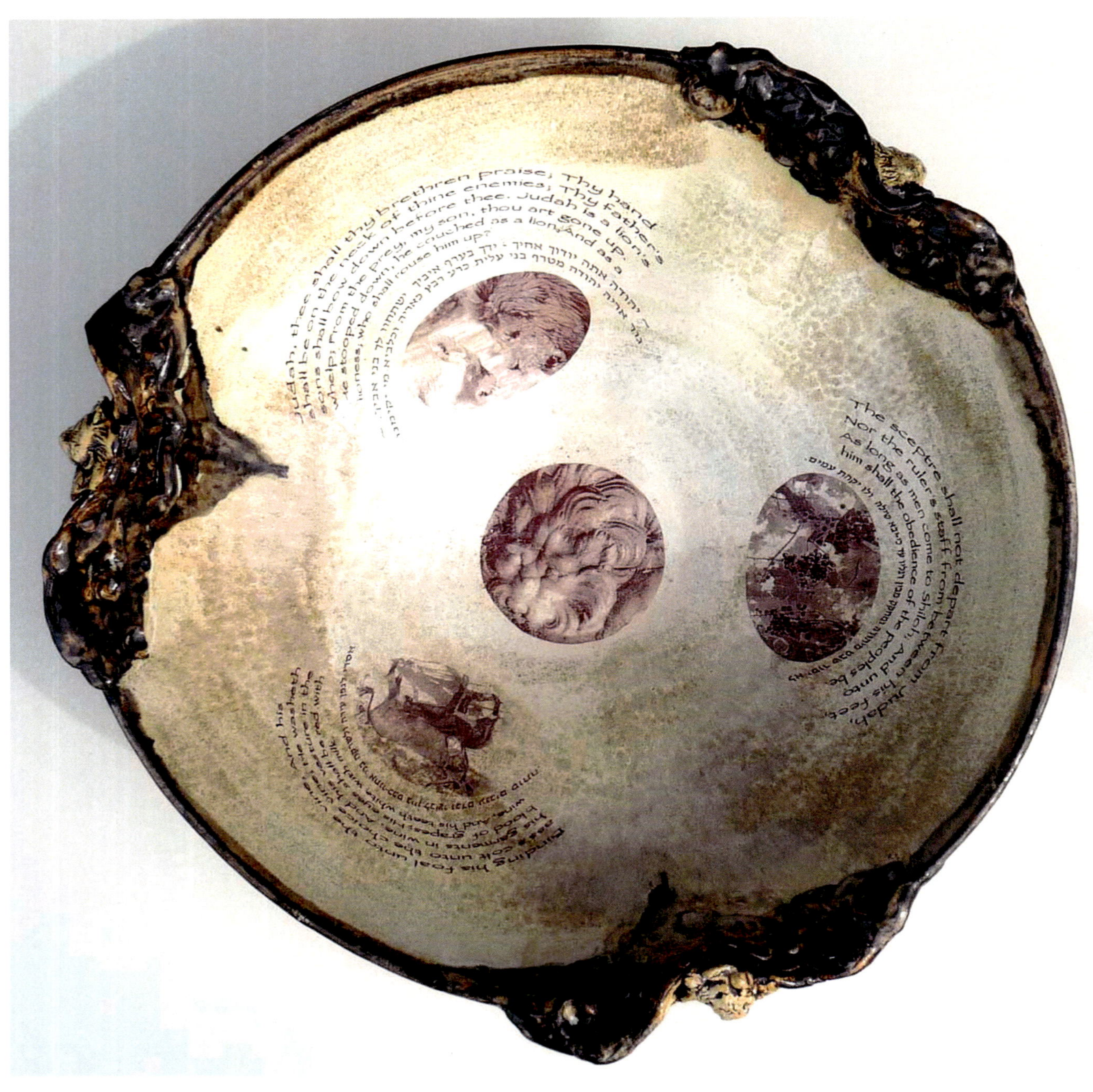

Judah (17 in. width x 6 in. height)

"Judah, thee shall thy brethren praise; thy hand shall be on the neck of thine enemies; thy father's sons shall bow down before thee. Judah is a lion's whelp; from the prey, my son, thou art gone up. He stooped down, he couched as a lion, and as a lioness; who shall rouse him up? The sceptre shall not depart from Judah, nor the ruler's staff from between his feet, as long as men come to Shiloh; and unto him shall the obedience of the peoples be. Binding his foal unto the vine, and his ass's colt unto the choice vine; he washeth his garments in wine, and his vesture in the blood of grapes; His eyes shall be red with wine, and his teeth white with milk." –Genesis 49:8-12

Jacob's blessing over Judah has been translated in several different ways, particularly the phrase shown here as: "until men come to Shiloh…" This is given in the King James version as "until Shiloh come." It can be taken either way, with Shiloh as subject or object. Such ambiguity is not unusual for poetry, which is usually the genre into which prophecy falls. What is not explicit is the meaning of "Shiloh." We know that it appears later in the books of Joshua and Judges as a place name where the ark and the tabernacle remained and where people came to sacrifice until it was conquered by the Philistines. It has been positively identified with an archaeological tel located 29 miles north of Jerusalem. Though the word "shiloh" and the word "shalom" are not related, many Jewish as well as Christian commentators interpret it as a messianic prophecy. Interestingly, the place name "Shiloh" is spelled differently in different books of the Bible. In an alternative spelling which appears in Judges, Psalms, and Jeremiah, the verse could mean, "until tribute comes to him." *Shi* translates as "tribute," *lo* translates as "to him." This would fit in terms of both meaning and style, utilizing the ancient Hebrew poetic device of parallelism: which which the stanza begins:

> *"The scepter shall not depart from Judah*
> *Nor the ruler's staff from between his feet,*
> *So that tribute shall come to him*
> *and the homage of the people be his."*

This raises the issue of scribal inconsistencies, even though the spelling of Shiloh is consistent within each of the seven books in which it is named. Although not held to the same standard of inerrancy, both the American Constitution and the Declaration of Independence contain inconsistencies in spelling, particularly in the names of people and places. In the final analysis, the last line of the stanza concerning the homage of the people could refer to the united kingdom of Israel under David and Solomon or to a messianic era in which all people shall pay homage, or both.

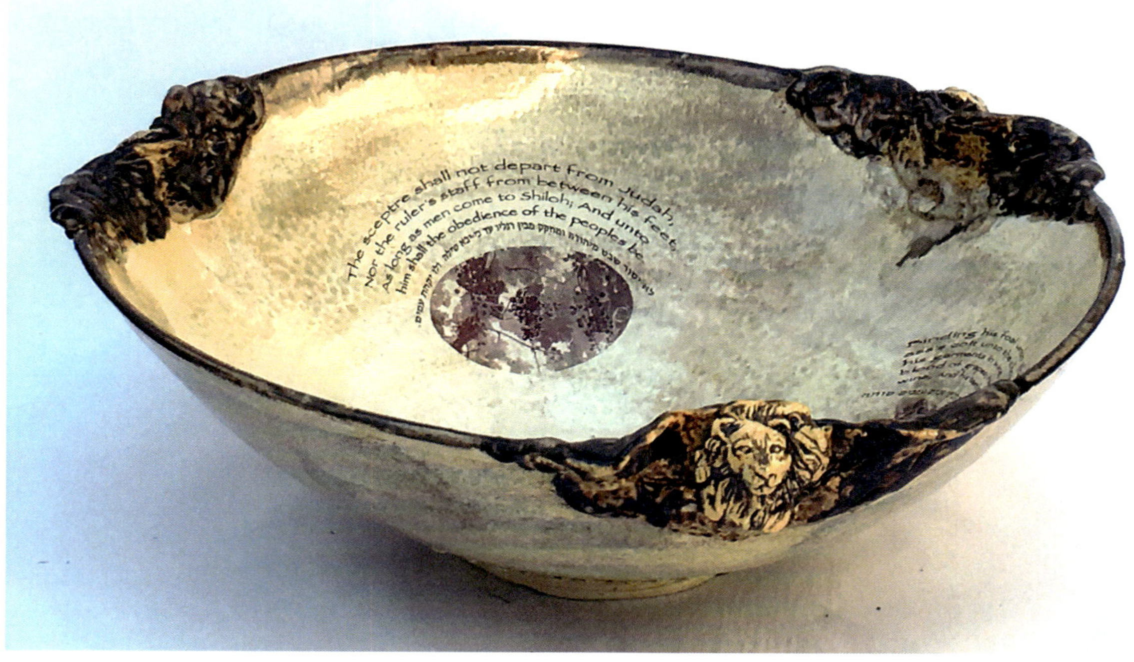

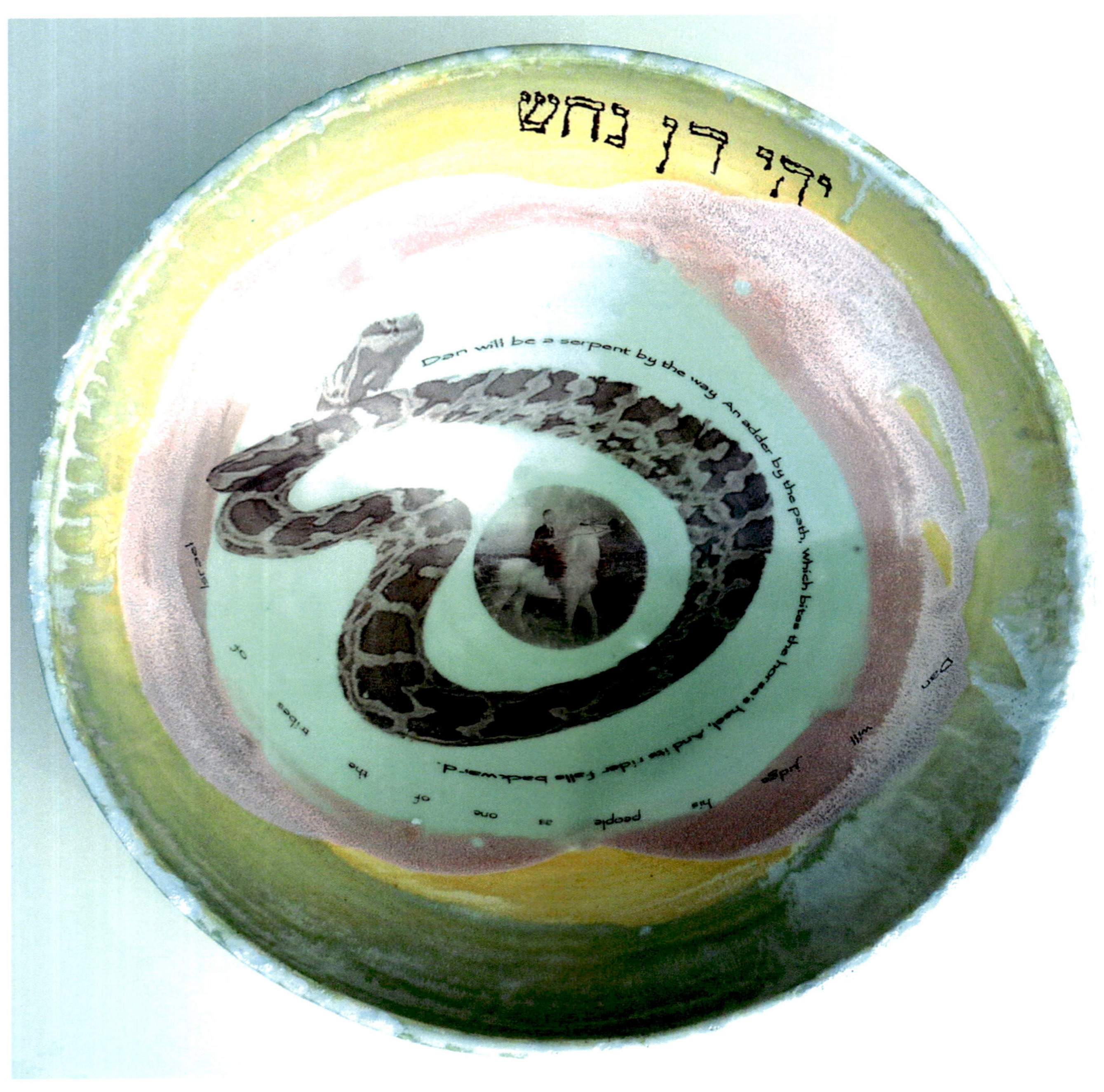

Dan (15 in. width x 5 ½ in. height)

"Dan will judge his people, as one of the tribes of Israel. Dan will be a serpent by the way, an adder by the path which bites the horse's heel, and his rider falls backward." – Genesis 49:16,17

Dan was the next son born to Jacob. After Leah bore four sons, Rachel, who was still barren, gave her handmaid Bilhah as a wife to her husband. Dan was the first child born to Bilhah. However, in his "blessings" over his sons, the next one mentioned was Zebulun followed by Isaachar. Indeed, birth order and primogeniture are often overturned in the Bible. Jacob himself was born following his twin brother Esau. Neither Joseph, Ephraim, Moses, or David were the firstborn. What was overturned much more rarely was the agency, or lack of agency, of women. Dinah, Jacob's only daughter, is given neither blessing nor tribal inheritance.

Though the birth order of Jacob's sons is reflected in the traditional Judaica representations, it is also not followed in Moses' blessings over the tribes. As to the order of the tribes that were inscribed on the precious and semi-precious stones of the High Priest's breastplate, there has been much speculation, but it is unknown. As if the above two sentences were not enough of a non sequitur, they are followed by the plea, "I have waited for thy salvation, O Lord." It is not clear whether this applies to the prophesy over Dan or whether it is simply Jacob's interjecting a short prayer, or whether it applies to Gad in the short blessing to follow. The word "dan" means judge in Hebrew. This is a contrast. A judge should be straightforward. A snake is sneaky.

On the bowl, Chaim was photographed on the white horse by Yonnah at Kibbutz Gezer, an ancient site in Israel. The picture depicts the horse and rider a moment before the prophesied mishap.

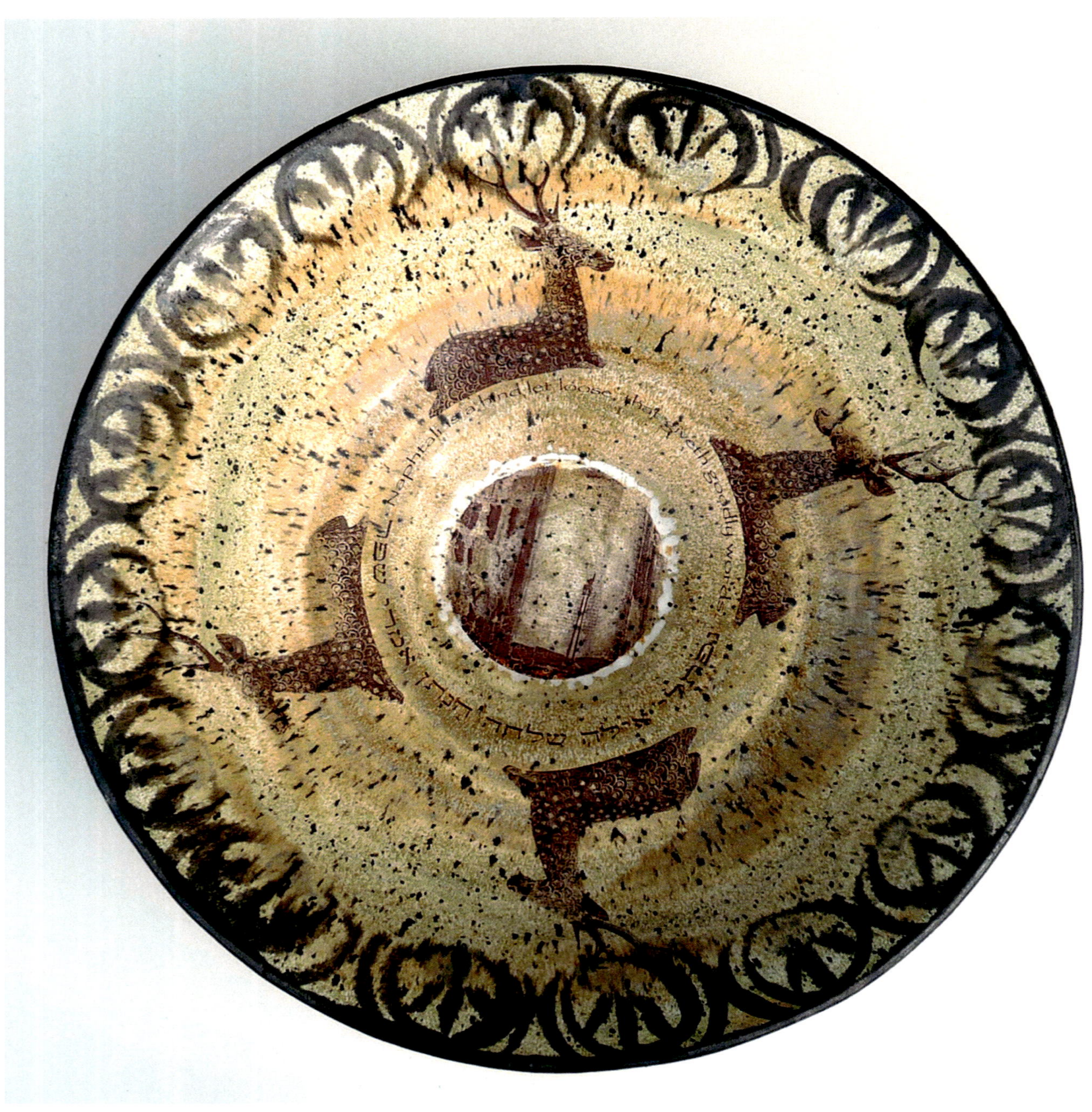

Naphtali (18 in. width x 5 ½ in. height)

"Naphtali is a hind let loose, that giveth goodly words." – Genesis 49:21

The center shows a scroll with a ceremonial pointer, called a yod (hand), and a Torah scroll. This symbolizes the phrase "goodly words." However, the word usually translated as "words" is sometimes translated, as in the Jerusalem Bible, as "fawns." Moses' blessing over the tribe in Deuteronomy 33 has also been subjected to several interpretations. The King James reads: "O Naphtali, satisfied with favour, and full with the blessing of the LORD: possess thou the west and the south." In Hebrew it reads "sea and south," which could refer to region of the Sea of Galilee the allotted territory of Naphtali.

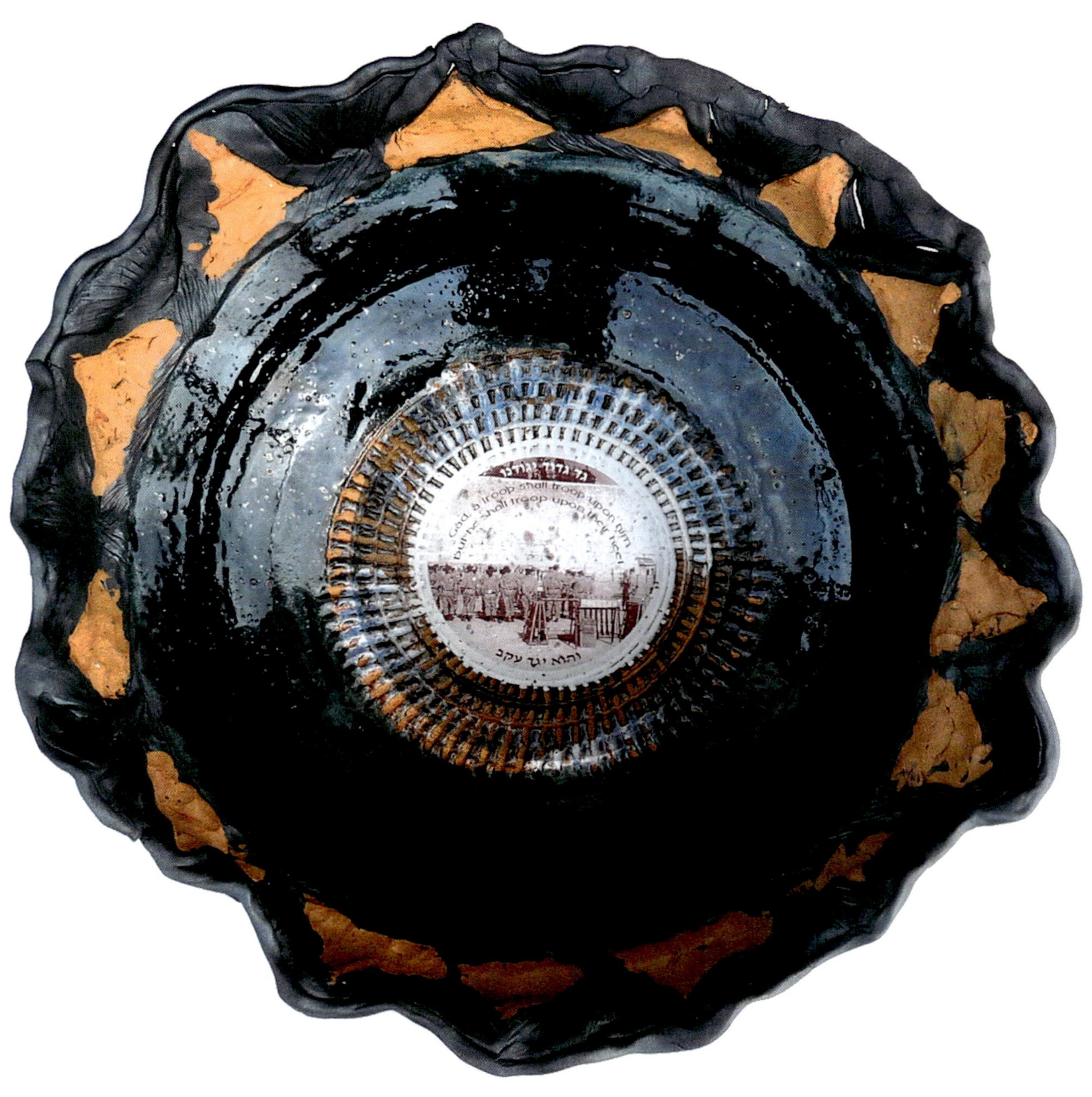

Gad (17 in. width x 8 in. height)

"Gad, a troop shall troop upon him but he shall troop upon their heel." – Genesis 49:16,17

Gad is the first son born to Leah's maidservant, Zilpah. Upon his birth, Leah exclaimed, "What good fortune!" Luck or fortune is the literal meaning of the name. It was also the name of a Semitic god of fortune, the worship of which which Isaiah mentions in his chastisements of Israel (Isaiah 65:11). In his blessing, Jacob makes a play on words. Gad sounds like the Hebrew word for troop, *"gdood."* Jacob's blessing has the cadence of a limerick or march. *"Gad gdood ygoodenoo v'hoo yagood akev."* It is full of assonance. On the bowl paratroopers are being inducted at the Western Wall; each receives a Bible and a rifle.

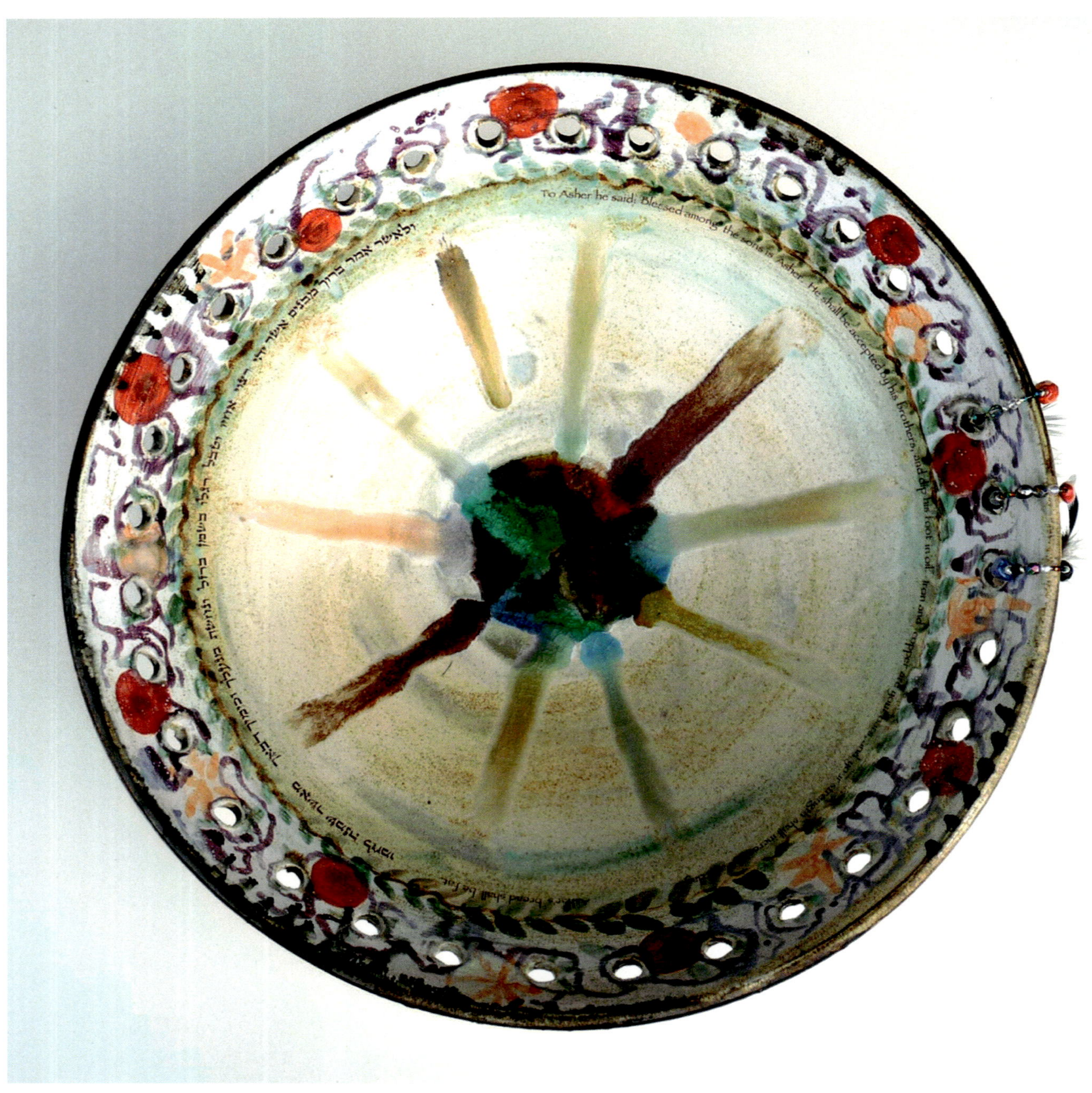

Asher (16 in. width x 6 in. height)

"Asher's bread shall be fat. He shall yield royal dainties." – Genesis 49:20 "

"Blessed among the sons is Asher. He shall be accepted by his brothers, and dip his foot in oil. Iron and copper are your bars, and your strength shall increase each day." – Deuteronomy 33:24,25

Asher, meaning happy, was the second son born to Zilpah. The bars of iron and copper and the pool of oil are represented by the central design, which was achieved by melting colored glass into the glaze. The perimeter design represents whatever delicacies are hinted at in the passage from Genesis.

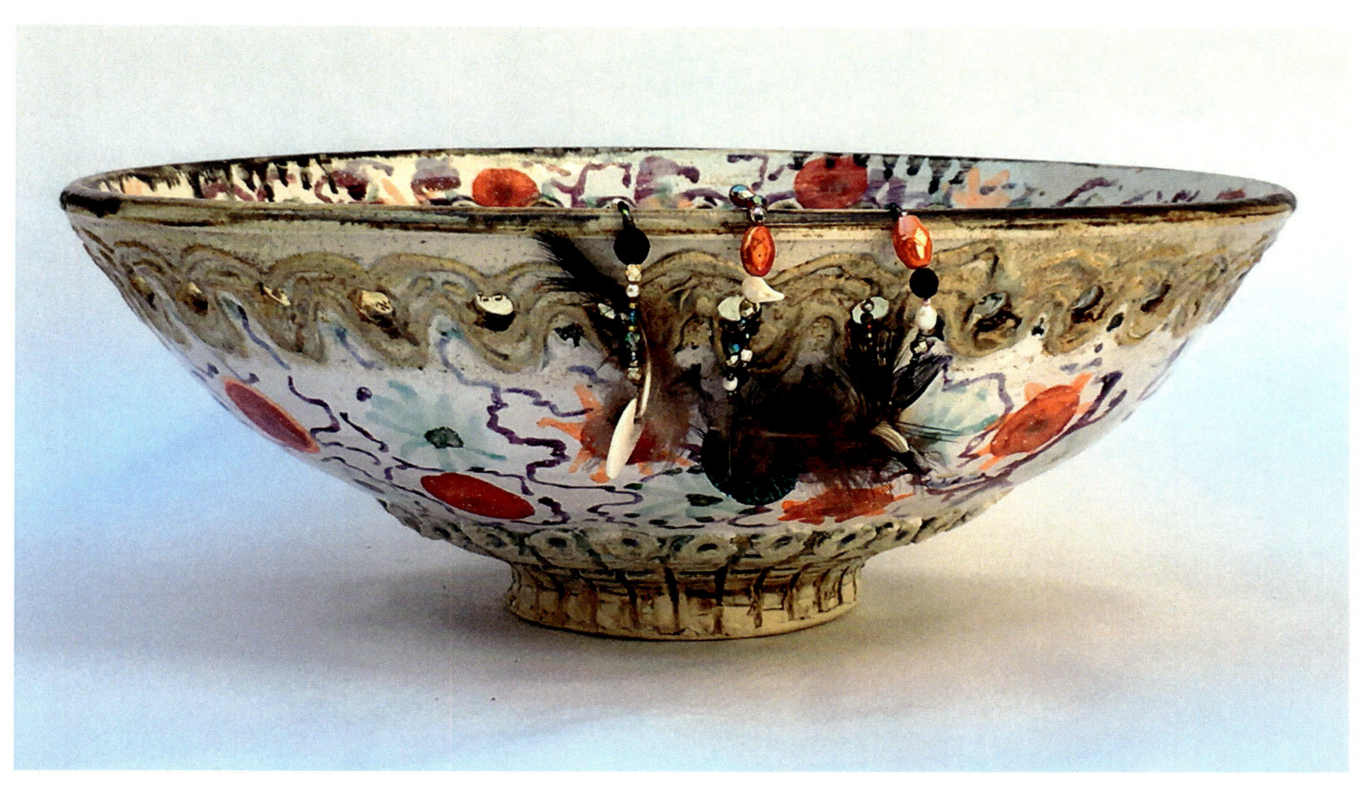

Asher (exterior)

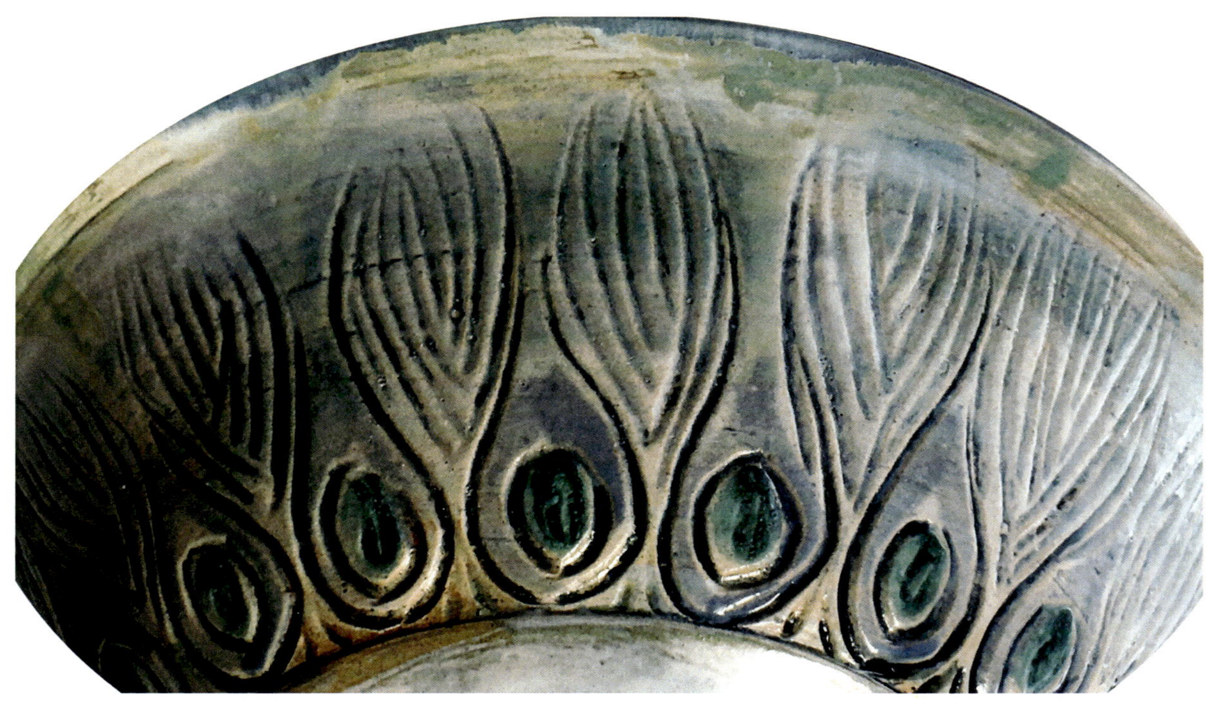

Issachar (exterior)

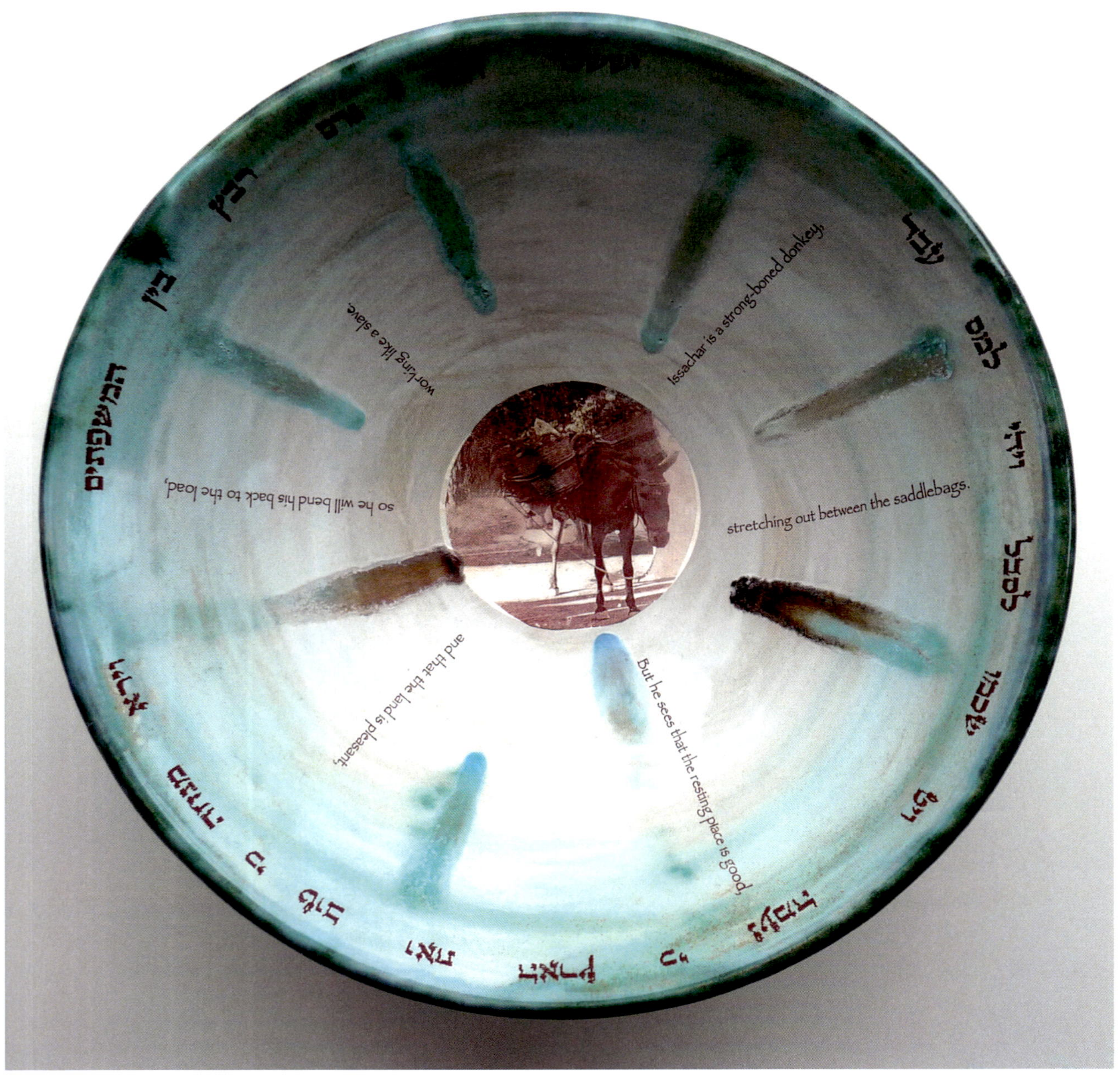

Issachar (17 in. width x 6 in. height)

"Issachar is a strong boned donkey stretching out between the saddlebags. But he sees that the resting place is good and that the land is pleasant, so he will bend his back to the load, working like a slave." – Genesis 49:14,15

Leah's naming of Issachar may derive from the Hebrew *ish socher* meaning hired man. In Jacob's blessing "slave" denotes a humble destiny. "He bent down to suffer forced labor," not just as a slave, but literally as a tax or bond slave." A few chapters ahead in Exodus, the original Hebrew for "taskmaster" is literally tax master. To quote Benjamin Franklin: "In this world nothing can be said to be certain, except death and taxes. In fact, it was the issue of taxes and forced labor that later caused the northern tribes, including Issachar, to secede.

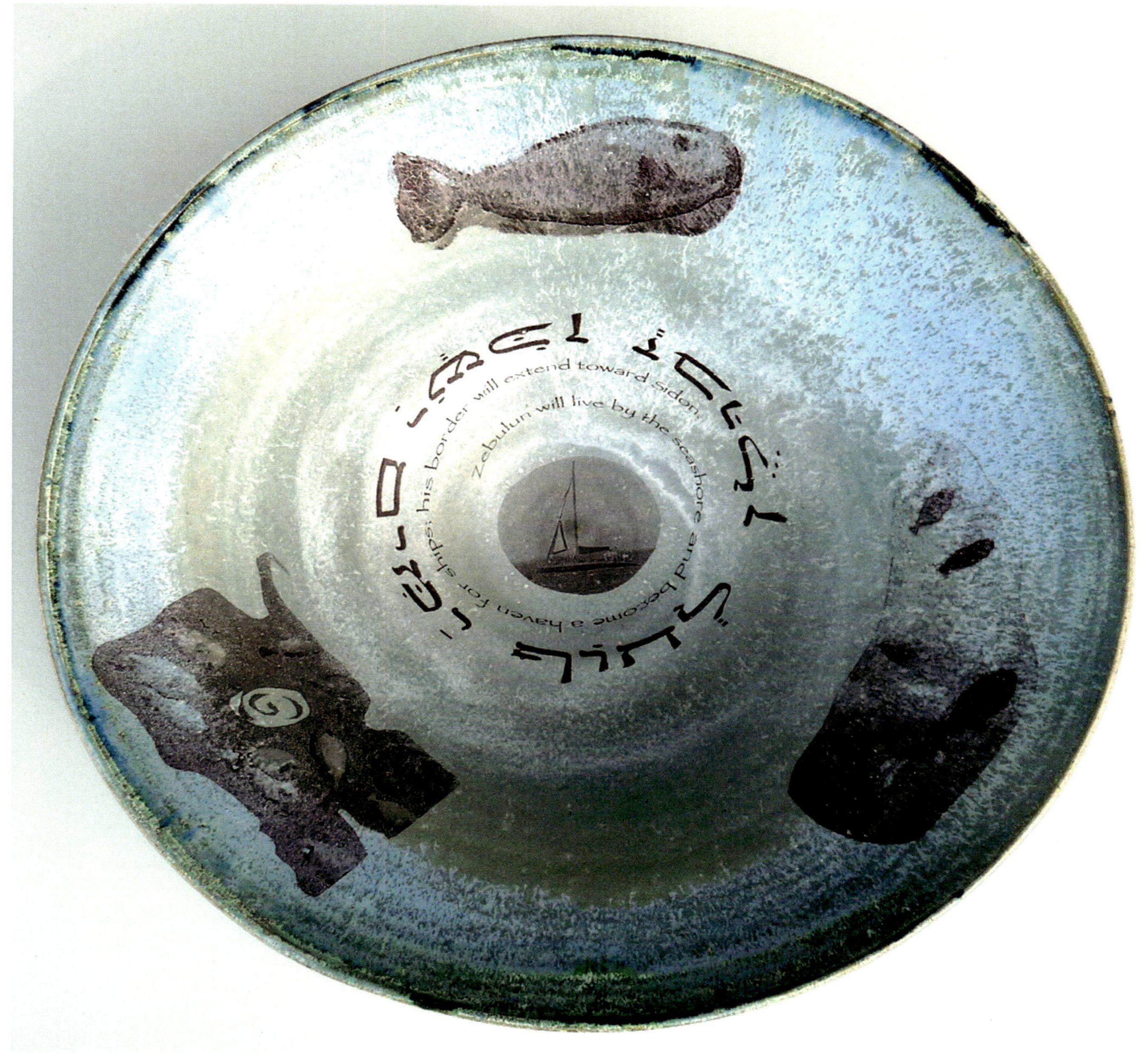

Zebulun (16 in. width x 6 in. height)

"Zebulun will live by the seashore and become a haven for ships: his border will extend toward Sidon." – Genesis 49:13

Unlike the other blessings of Jacob or of Moses, Zebulun's is exclusively concerned with geography, even naming the Phoenician port city of Sidon as a reference point. Despite the seagoing references, when the territories were allotted Zebulun's did not extend to the sea; it was landlocked. Nevertheless, the bowl's color and imagery reflect the sea.

After her last son, Leah gave birth to Dinah, the only daughter, and the only name for which no etymology is given. However, "Dinah" shares the same root as "Dan." It is the feminine form of judgment, relevant in light of what happened to her in Shechem, and its repercussions.

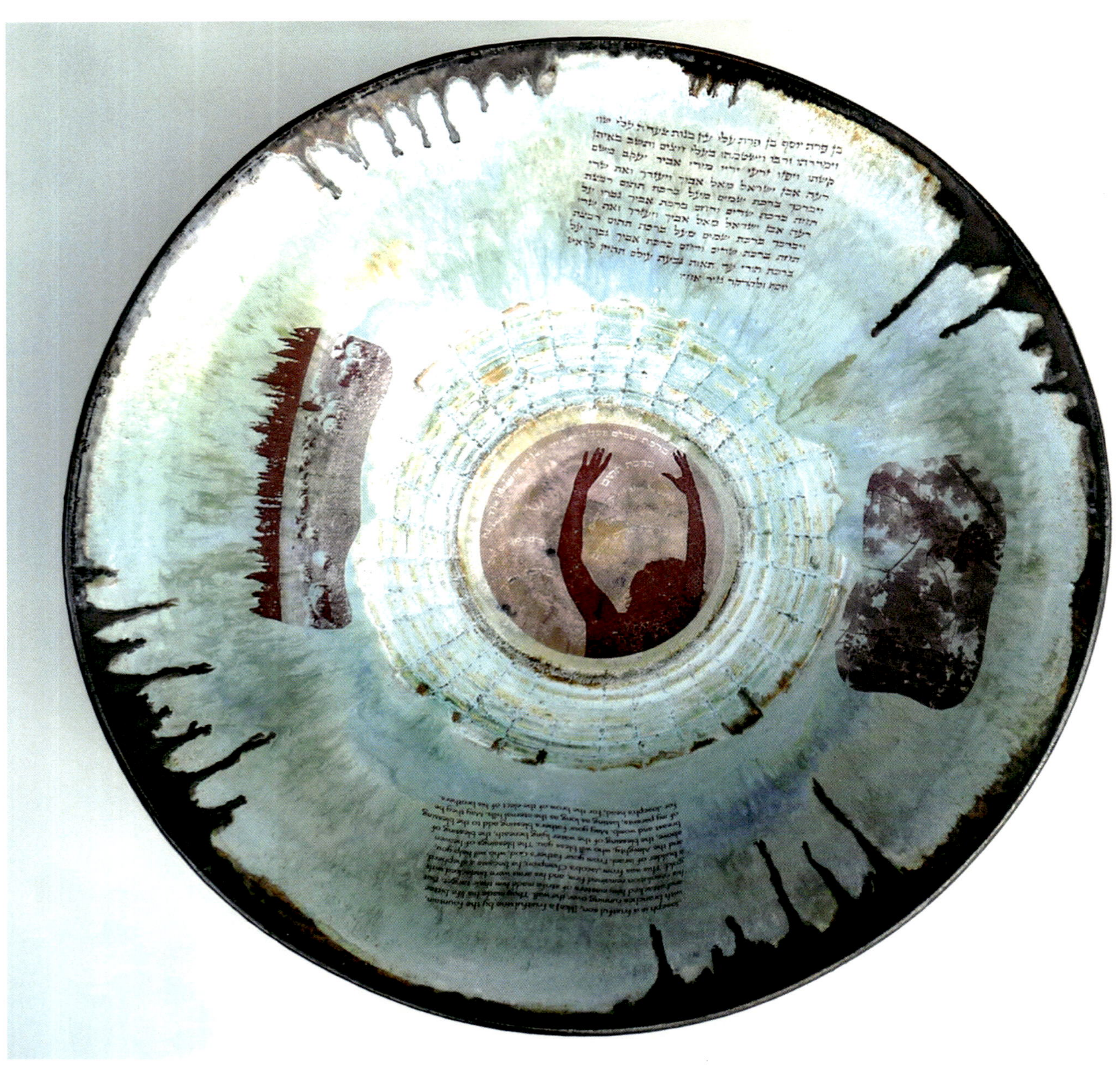

Joseph (18 in. width x 5 ½ in. height)

"Joseph is a fruitful vine, a fruitful vine by a fountain; its branches run over the wall. The archers have dealt bitterly with him, and shot at him, and hated him; But his bow abode firm, and the arms of his hands were made supple, by the hands of the Mighty One of Jacob, from thence, from the Shepherd, the Stone of Israel, Even by the God of thy father, who shall help thee, and by the Almighty, who shall bless thee, with blessings of heaven above, blessings of the deep that coucheth beneath, blessings of the breasts, and of the womb. The blessings of thy father are mighty beyond the blessings of my progenitors unto the utmost bound of the everlasting hills; they shall be on the head of Joseph, and on the crown of the head of the prince among his brethren." – Genesis 49:22-26

The lyricism of this passage and the length of it attest to Jacob's special love for Joseph, Rachel's first son, so the blessing is included in its entirety in the bowl. It includes both maternal and paternal blessings. Blessings from the heavens (heaven is plural in Hebrew) and blessings from the earth. The central image shows a silhouette with hands raised to heaven and words in Hebrew and English emanating like leaves from a date tree: "The blessing of heaven above. The blessing of the deep and the womb." The other images show a shepherd with his sheep from a photograph taken near Hadera, Israel, and grapes in a vineyard photographed in Ein Karem, which means "spring of the vineyard."

In the previous chapter of Genesis, as Jacob lay on his deathbed, before uttering his blessings over his sons, Joseph presents his sons, Manasseh and Ephraim. Jacob's adoption of Joseph's two sons gave Joseph a double portion, which is effectively a birthright. The nearly blind Jacob adopts Joseph's two sons as his own children and then, as he reaches out to lay his hands upon them in blessing, crosses his hands, giving preeminence to Ephraim, the younger brother. As it turned out, though the blessing went to Ephraim, the birthright did go to the older child, Manasseh, who was to inherit territories on both sides of the Jordan. However, the tribe of Manasseh was never able to conquer the entire territory from the Canaanites.

The territory of Ephraim sat strategically in what was to become the center of Samaria, between the smaller tribe of Benjamin and the weaker tribe of Manasseh. In fact, just as Jacob is sometimes referred to as Israel, the confederacy of the northern tribes, which was to break away and establish a separate kingdom, is often referred to as Ephraim. Jeroboam and successive kings who reigned in Samaria were of the tribe of Ephraim. It seems that the competition and jealousy among the brothers which had caused them to throw Joseph into a pit was reciprocated by Joseph's descendants as they established an alternative kingdom, capital, temples, and religion. But, aside from sibling rivalry, the breakup of the United Kingdom into Judah and Israel began, as mentioned before, as a tax revolt.

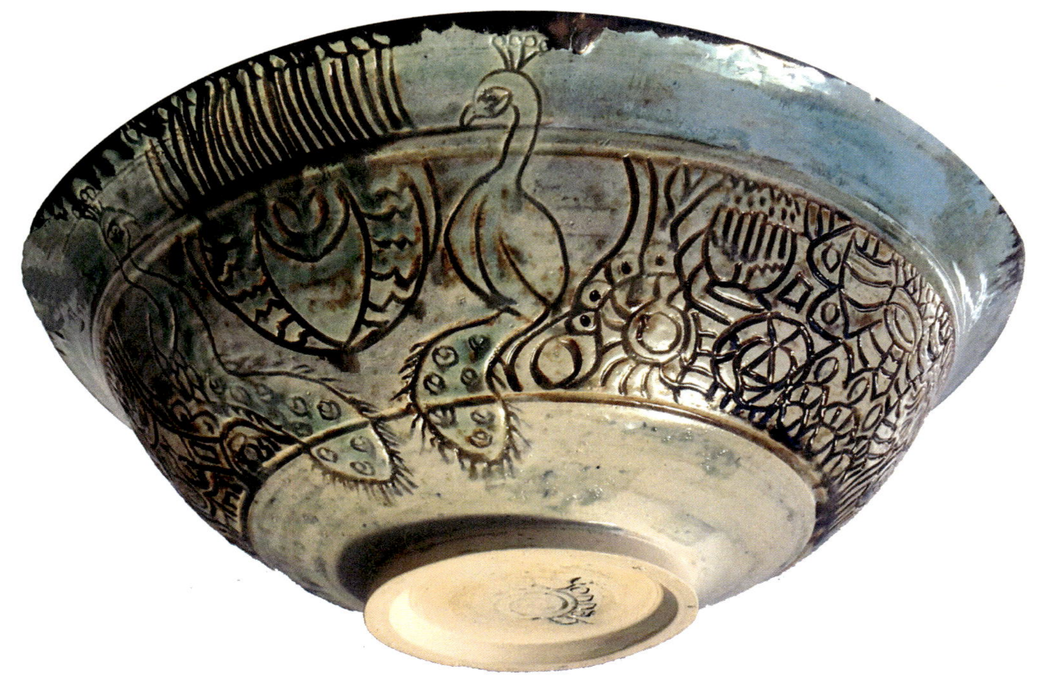

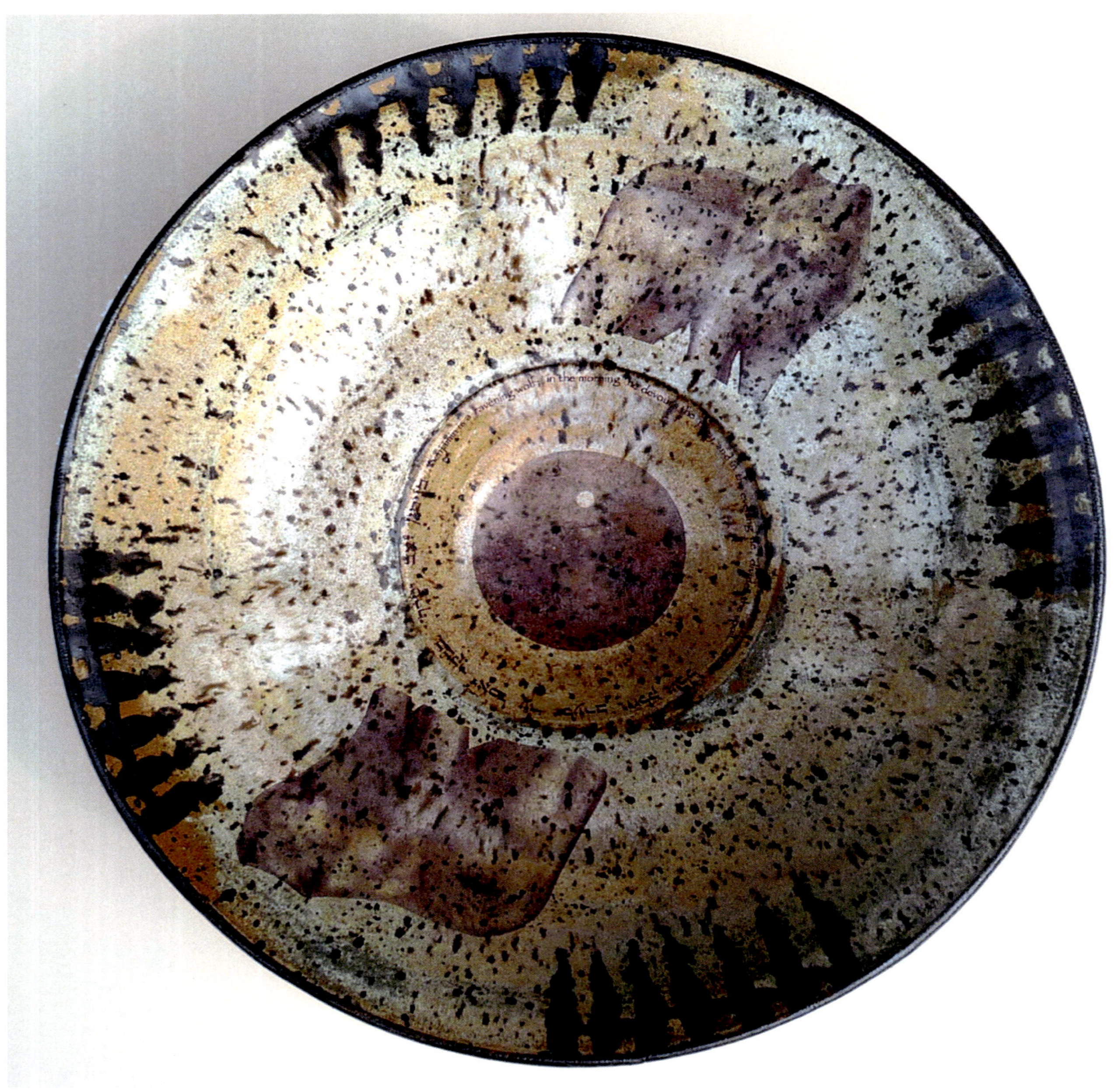

Benjamin (17 in. width x 5 ½ in. height)

"Benjamin is a ravening wolf; in the morning he devours the prey, and in the evening he divides the spoil." – Genesis 49:27

Rachel died giving birth to her second son in Bethlehem, where she is buried. She wanted to name him Benoni, meaning "son of my sorrow," but Jacob changed it to Benjamin, son of the right hand. Benjamin, both as an individual and as a tribe was singled out many times. When the brothers went down to Egypt to buy grain, they left Benjamin behind with their father, but Joseph, who was unrecognized by his brothers, asked leading questions to elicit the mention of the missing brother and then insisted that he be brought down. After acquiescing and returning with Benjamin, the brothers were put to the test, whether they dispense with Benjamin as they had with Joseph.

Later, the Book of Judges recounts a war – all of the tribes vs. Benjamin. The incident that precipitated the war is as follows: A Levite had a concubine who was gang raped by a group of Benjamites. She died and, desiring justice, the Levite cut up her body into twelve pieces and sending each tribe a body part. The outraged tribes approached the Tribe of Benjamin asking that the perpetrators be delivered, but their demand was refused. This resulted in the Battle of Gibeah. Twenty-five thousand Benjamites, including seven hundred who were ambidextrous fought again four hundred thousand men. As a result of the battle, the Tribe of Benjamin, including women and children, was decimated and nearly extinguished. The account of the three day battle, including strategy, is given in great detail.
Six hundred men of Benjamin survived by hiding in a cave. Saul, the first king of Israel, was descended from one of these men.

The men of Israel had vowed never to give their daughters in marriage to a Benjamite. Now that the tribe was almost wiped out, they realized that they did not want it to completely disappear. It was a demographic puzzle; how to find wives for the survivors so that they could regenerate the tribe? They decided to send an expeditionary force to the town of Jabeth-Gilead, which had not sent any volunteers to the battle. All of the men of the town and all of the women, except for four hundred virgins were put to the sword. These were presented as a good will gesture to the surviving Benjamites, however a couple of a hundred additional virgins were still needed.

Another plan was devised. There was an annual feast in Shiloh, The remaining Benjamite bachelors were instructed to hide in the vineyards until it was time for the virgins to dance in the field. Then each could grab himself a wife.

The same wolf is depicted twice on the bowl, a lone wolf. It was not easy to find a wolf but they can be found at Wolf Haven, an animal preserve outside of Olympia, Washington. The image in the center of the bowl is the moon rising over the trees.

Blessing over the Reading of the Torah selection from "Vayechi Suite"
for Recorder, Bassoon,Trumpet, Trombone, Harp, Timpani, and Voices

Chaim Bezalel

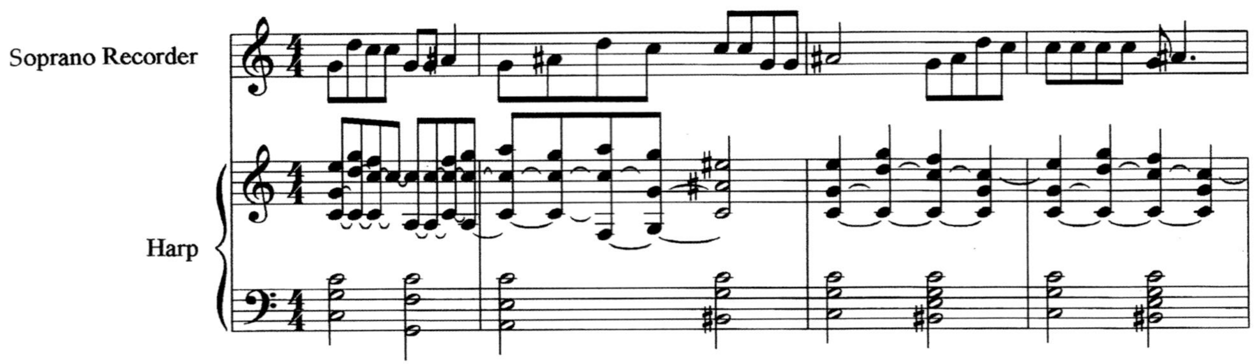

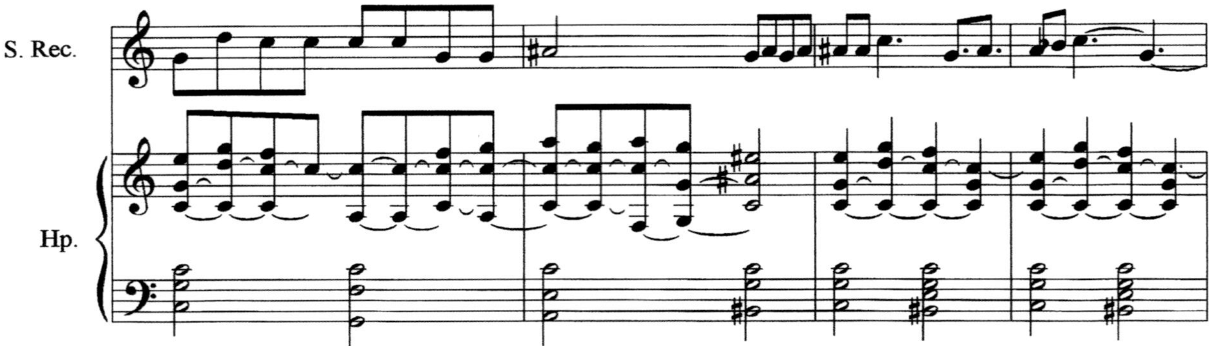

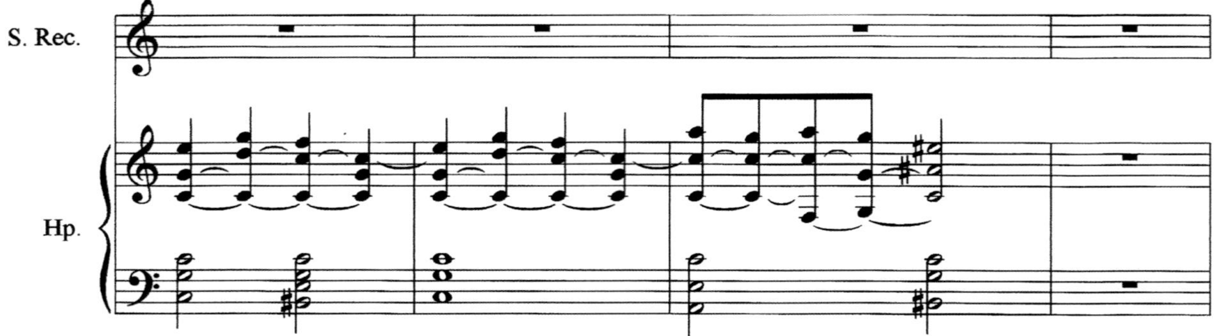

Urim and Thummim

"And thou shalt put in the breastplate of judgment the Urim and the Thummim; and they shall be upon Aaron's heart, when he goeth in before the LORD: and Aaron shall bear the judgment of the children of Israel upon his heart before the LORD continually." - Exodus 28:30

"And he shall stand before Eleazar the priest, who shall ask counsel for him after the judgment of Urim before the LORD: at his word shall they go out, and at his word they shall come in, both he, and all the children of Israel with him, even all the congregation." - Numbers 27:20-22

Nobody knows exactly what the Urim and Thummim were. They were hidden under the breastplate of the High Priest, with its array of twelve inlaid precious and semiprecious stones in their settings, each inscribed with the name of one of the twelve tribes of Israel. They served as an oracle through which the nation got direction and specific answers to their queries.

Some commentators believe that the Urim and Thummim consisted of the inscribed ineffable name of God (forbidden to be uttered but once a year by the High Priest). Some believe it was connected to the casting of lots. Others believe that they had no physical form at all but were integral to the breastplate itself. How the oracle operated is a mystery. The word *urim* can be translated as lights. The word *thummim* is the plural of innocent, simple, or honest - in modern Hebrew, naive. But the explicit meaning of the words is also a mystery.

This project was first presented as an exhibition at the Khan Museum in the city of Ashkelon, Israel in 1991. The museum itself is located in a historic, restored mosque. Its minaret can be seen on pages 28 and 29. The project was titled "Urim and Thummim" because it is based upon a series of twelve polyptychs (multi-image panels) each laid out in an array of twelve images, like the stones on the breastplate of the high priest. In its earliest stage, the collaboration consisted of Yonnah's painted borders, like illuminations, around Chaim's photographs. This was the basis of a line of greeting card sets which we published and marketed primarily in Israel and, through mail order, around the world.

In late 1990, the Gulf War began and Chaim was drafted into the Israeli army. Tourists disappeared and did not return for a while, so the card business suffered. A gallery in Tel Aviv, which had commissioned us to make silkscreen prints, backed out. One day Chaim photocopied a photograph onto a sheet of rice paper and brought it home to Yonnah asking, "Can you paint this while I take out the garbage?" It sold. Going door to door at night with a portfolio of new work that combined photography and painting, we got through that difficult time, and made some friends as well.

Yonnah has said that the project served as our own oracle in the early stages of our collaboration. Many of the images contained in the 144 photographs became the basis of other works, some of which are included in this book. Unless otherwise noted as being the work of the individual artists, the works illustrated on the following pages were produced by the collaboration.

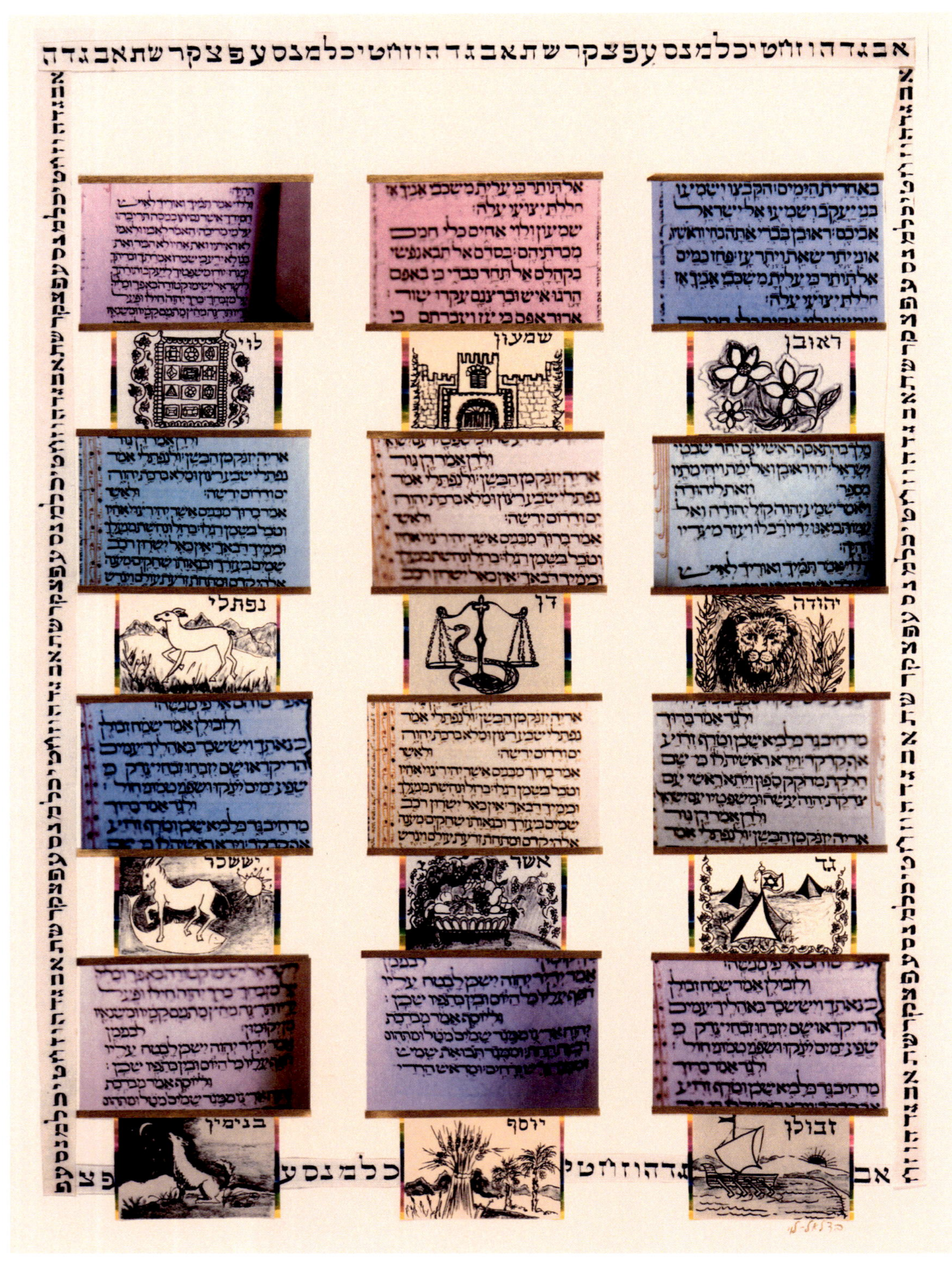

The Twelve Tribes (39 x 28 in.)

Photography, pen and ink on paper, and calligraphy on parchment. The photographs are of a 500 year old Hebrew Bible, one of the earliest printed books in Hebrew. From Genesis 49, these are Jacob's blessings over his sons.

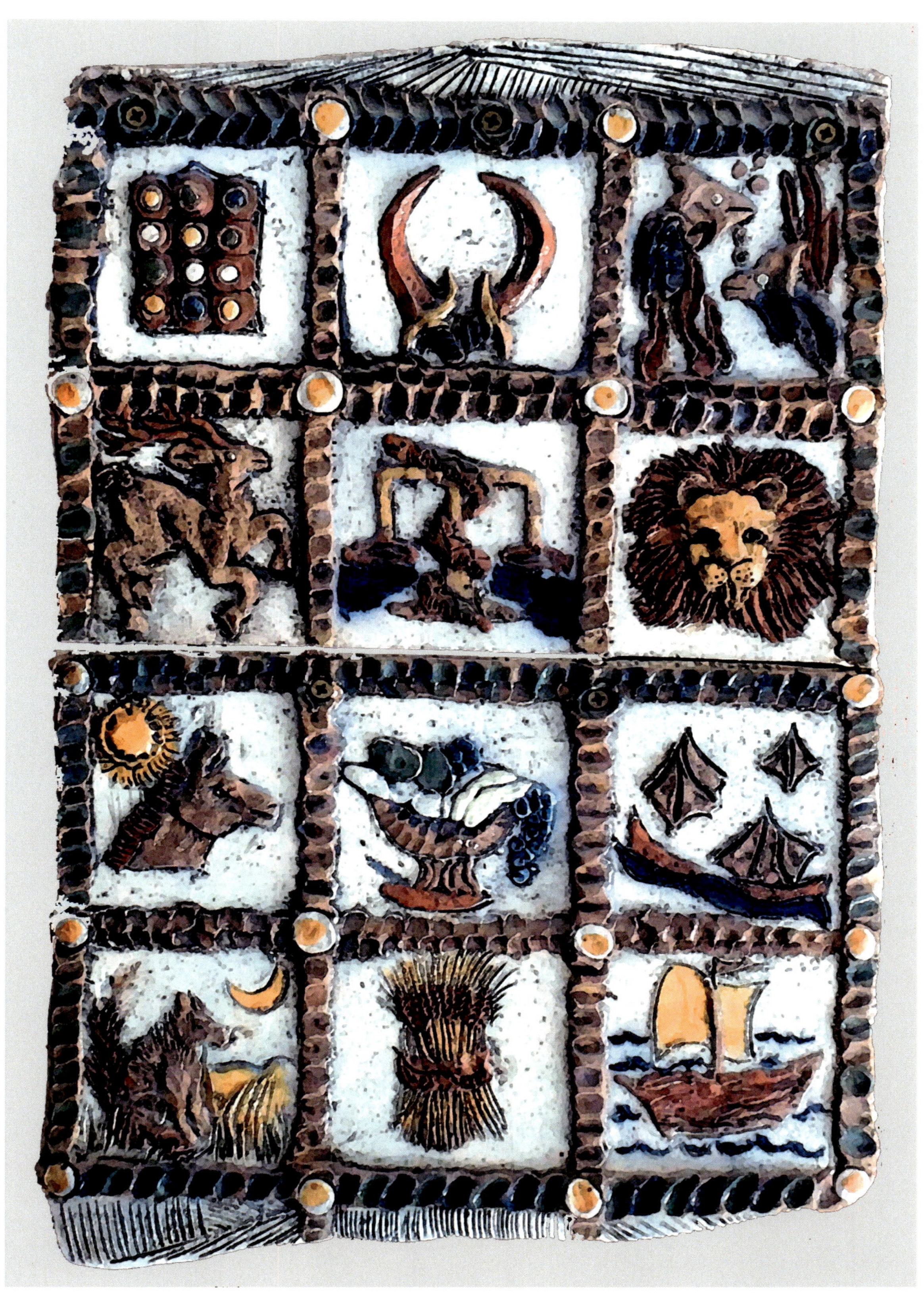

Twelve Tribes Plaque, *Yonnah Ben Levy* (1991) 17 x 13 in.

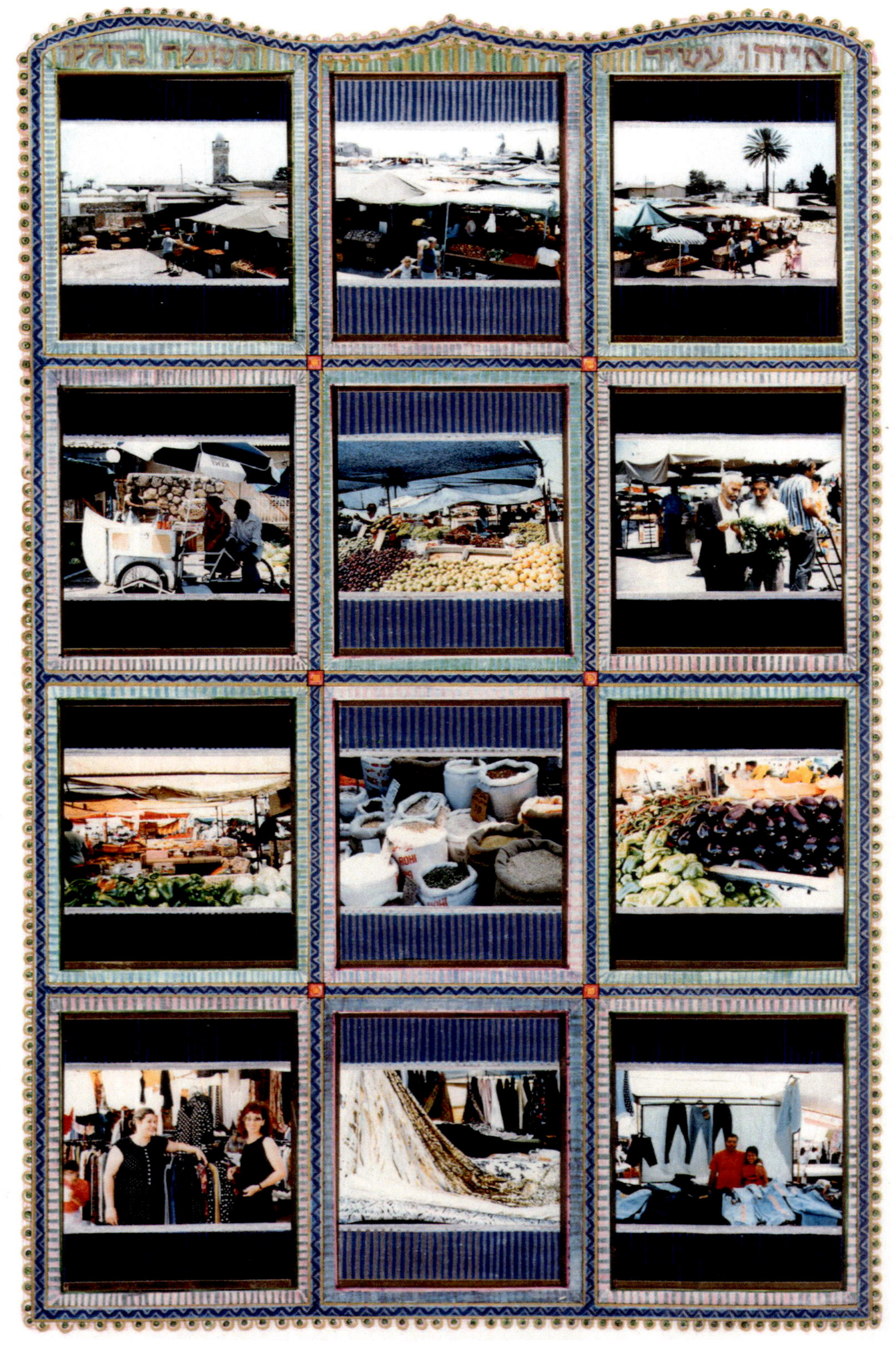

"Who is Rich? He who is happy with his lot." (36 x 22 in.)

This panel was the first completed in the series. The title, which is the superscription above, is from *Pirkei Avot*, "Ethics of the Fathers," a compilation of early Rabbinic ethical sayings. The photographs were taken at the outdoor market, or shuk, in Ashkelon, Israel.

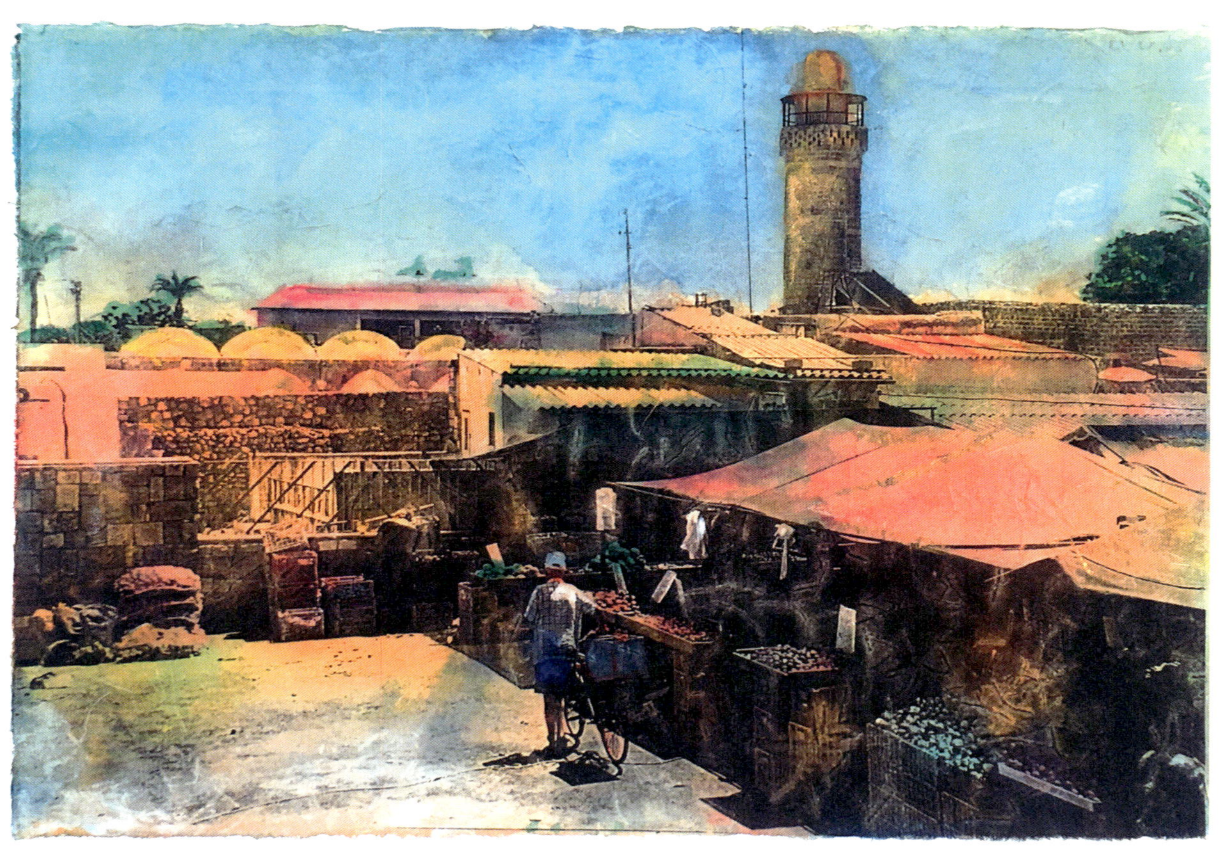

The Shuk I and II (1992) mixed-media on rice paper, 10 x 14 in. each

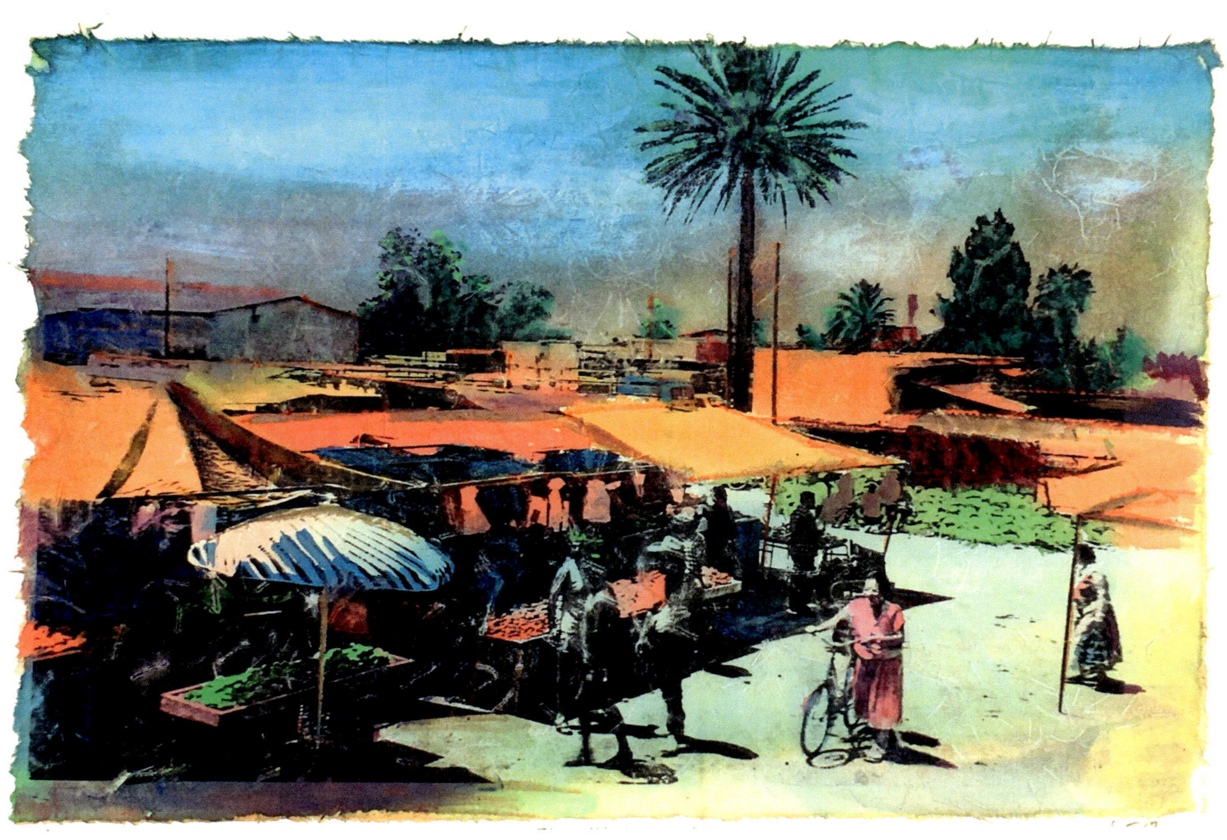

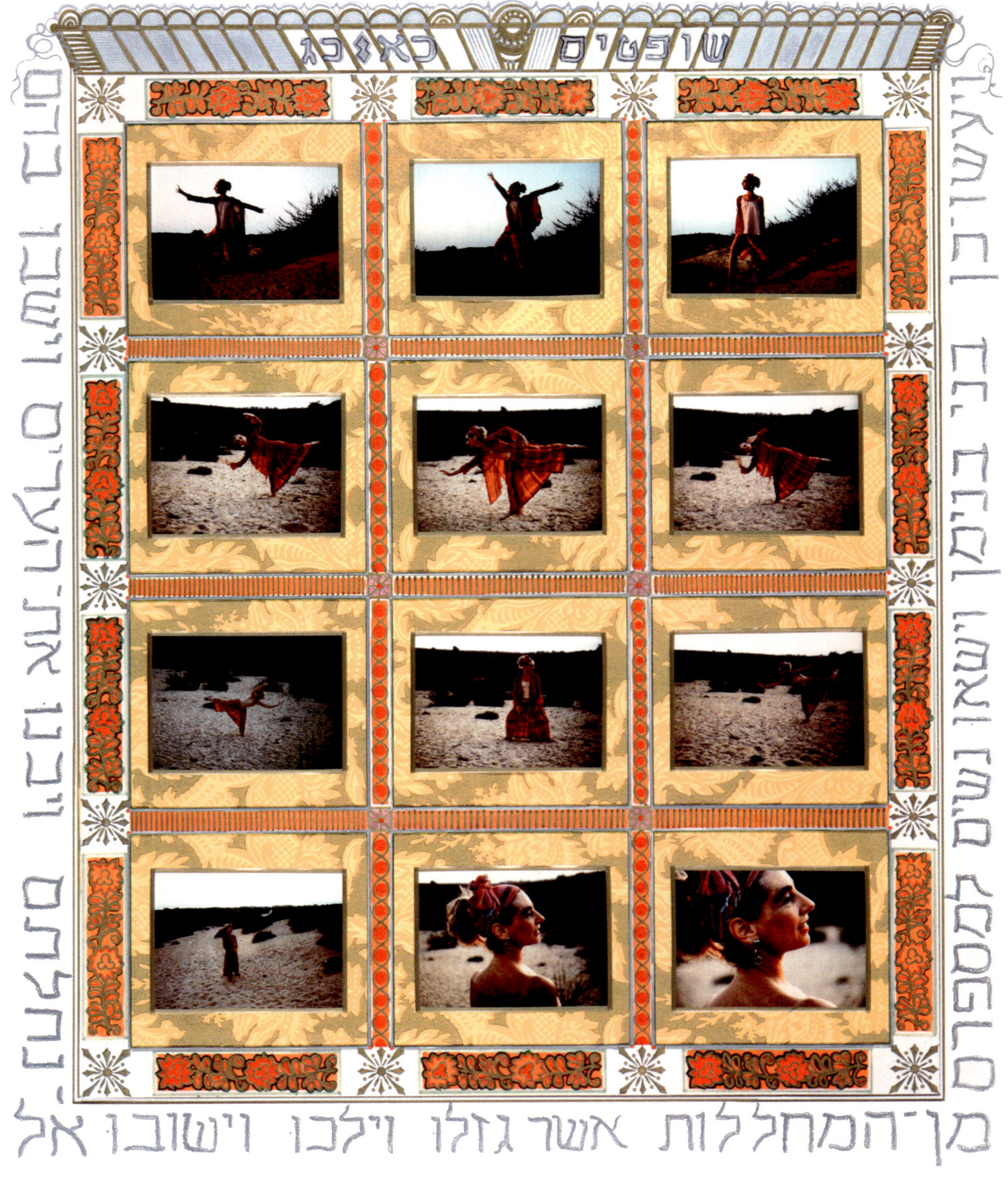

The Dancer (40 x 30 in.)

"And the children of Benjamin did so, and took them wives, according to their number, of them that danced, whom they caught: and they went and returned unto their inheritance, and repaired the cities, and dwelt in them." - Judges 21:23

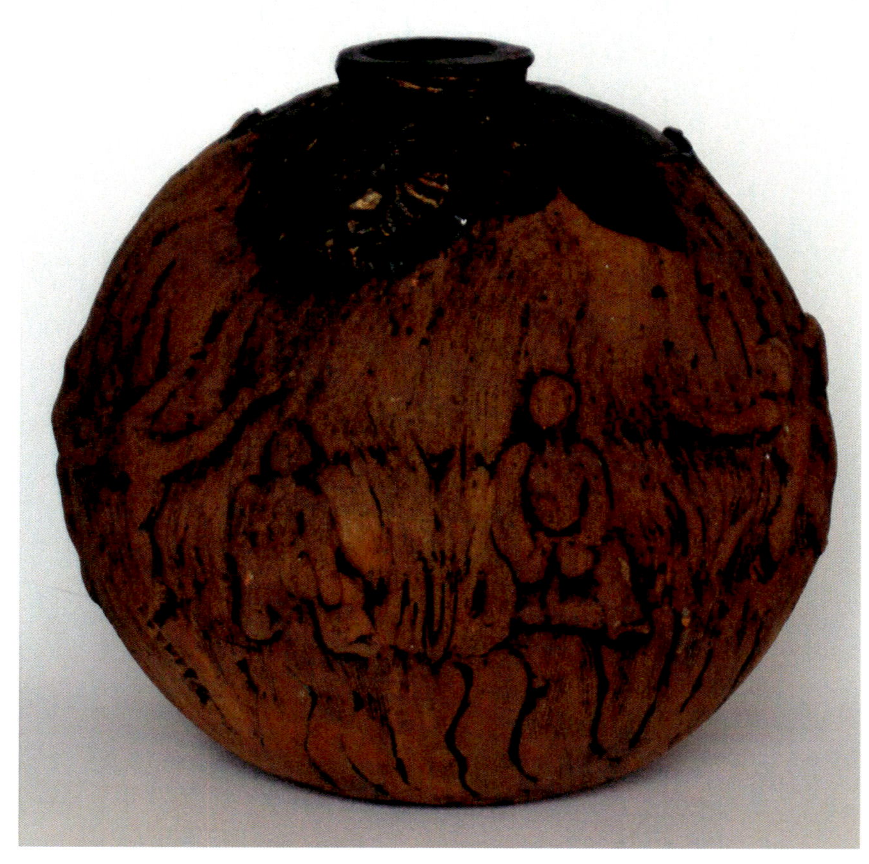

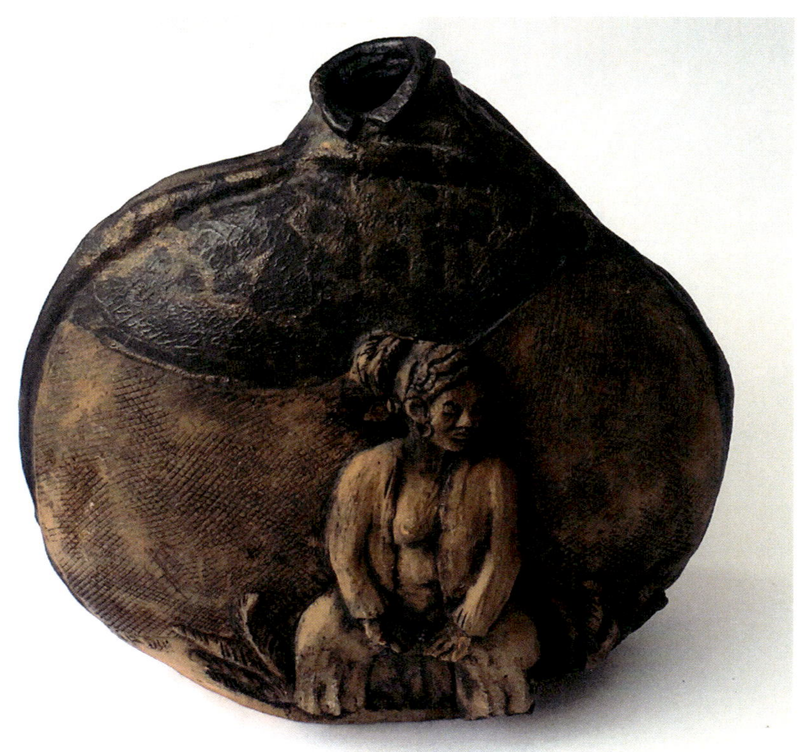

Two stoneware vessels by Yonnah Ben Levy (1991 & 1995)

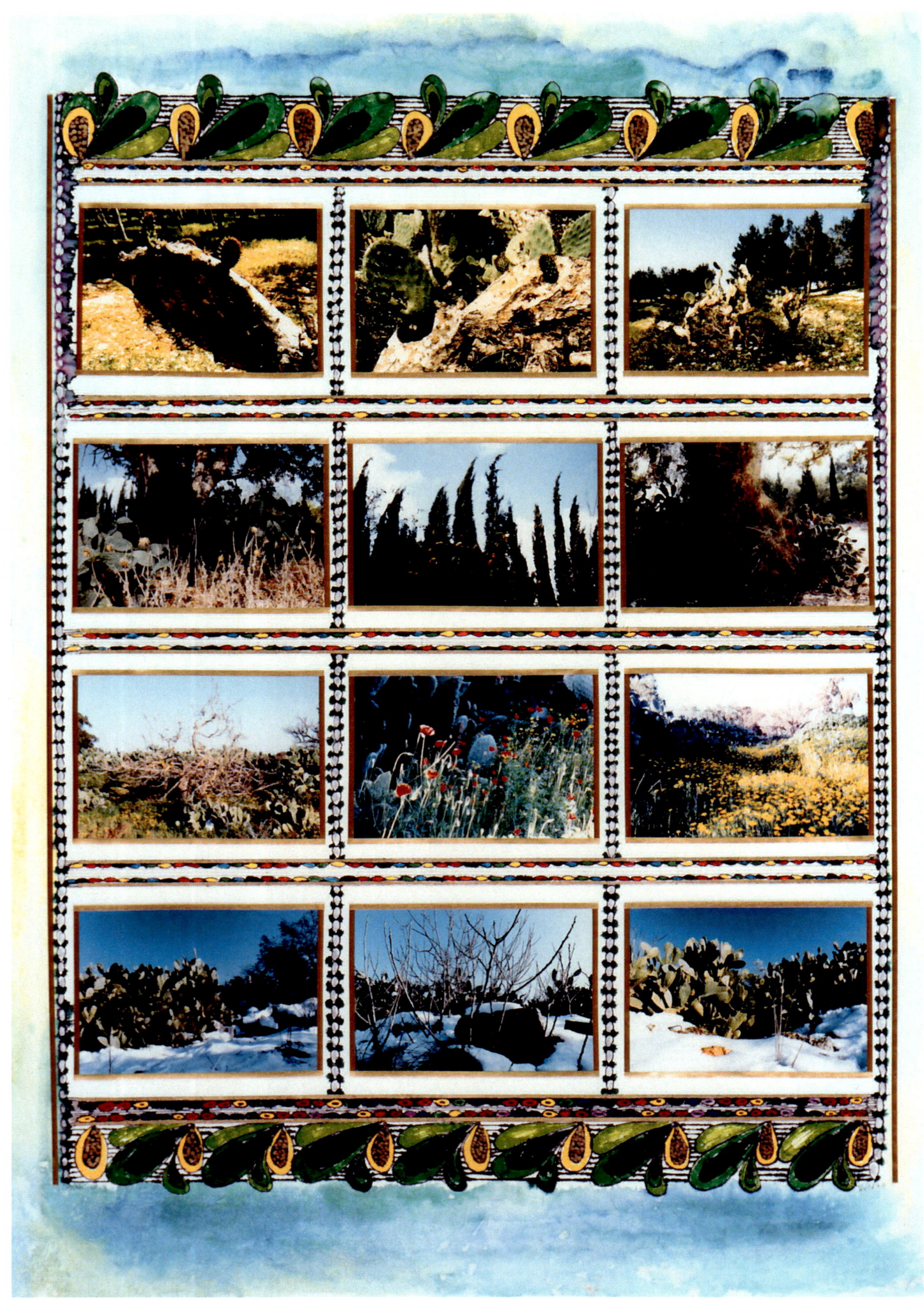

Sabras (40 x 28 in.)

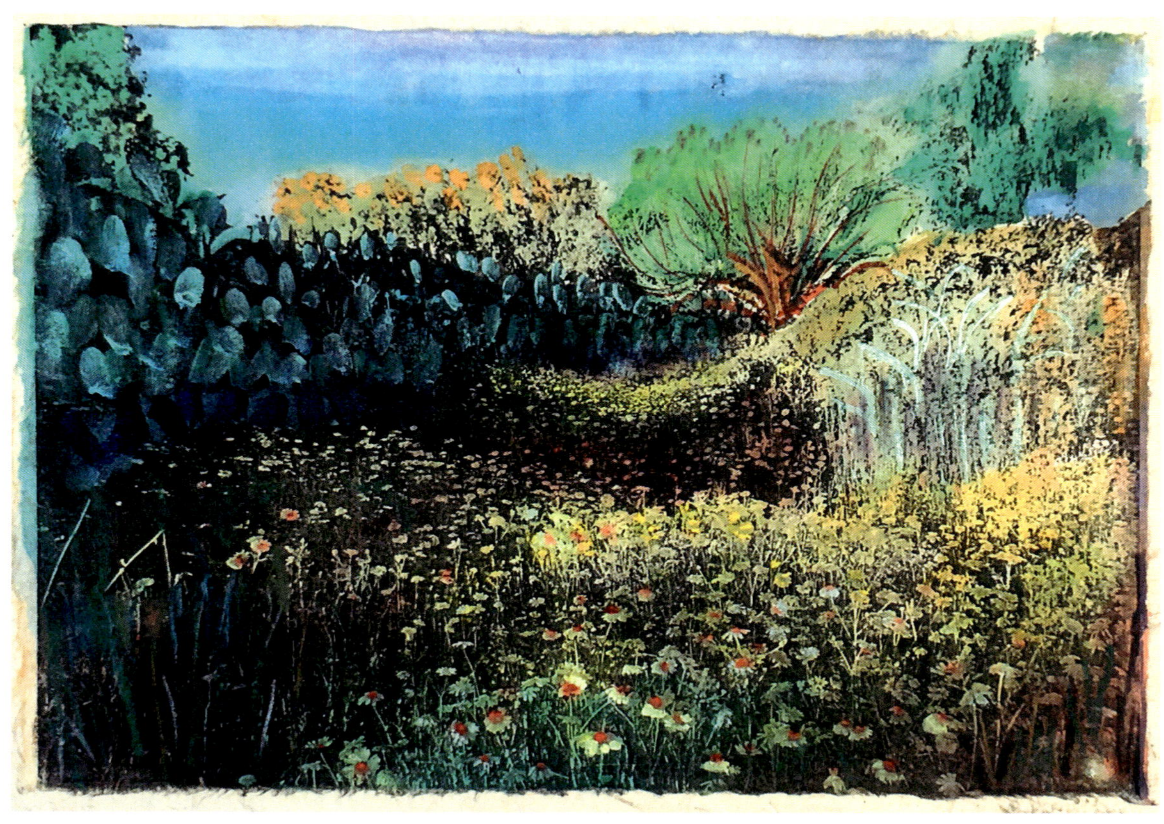

Sabras and Chamomile, mixed-media on rice paper (1992) 10 x 14 in.

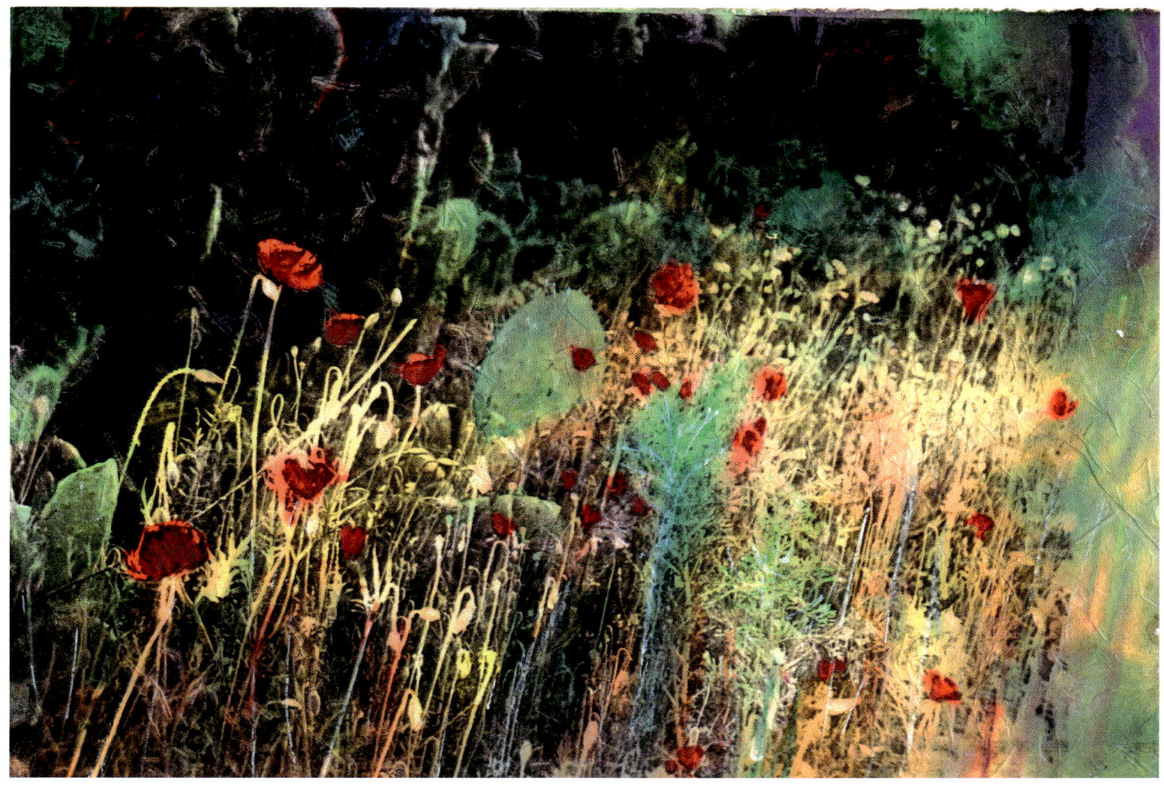

Sabras and Poppies, mixed-media on rice paper (1992) 10 x 14 in.

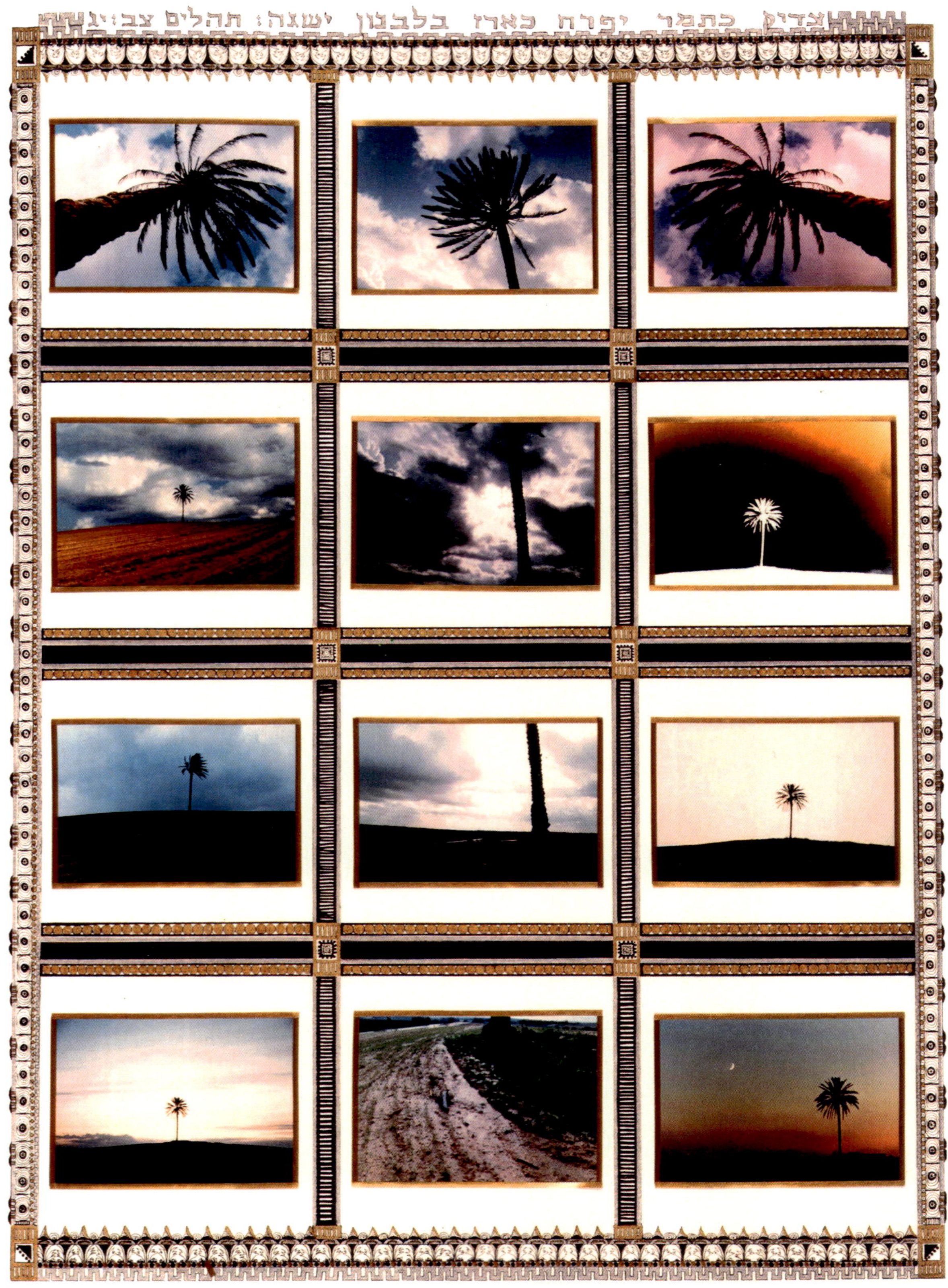

Palm Tree (40 x 28 in.)

"The righteous shall flourish like the palm tree: he shall grow like a cedar in Lebanon." -Psalm 92:12

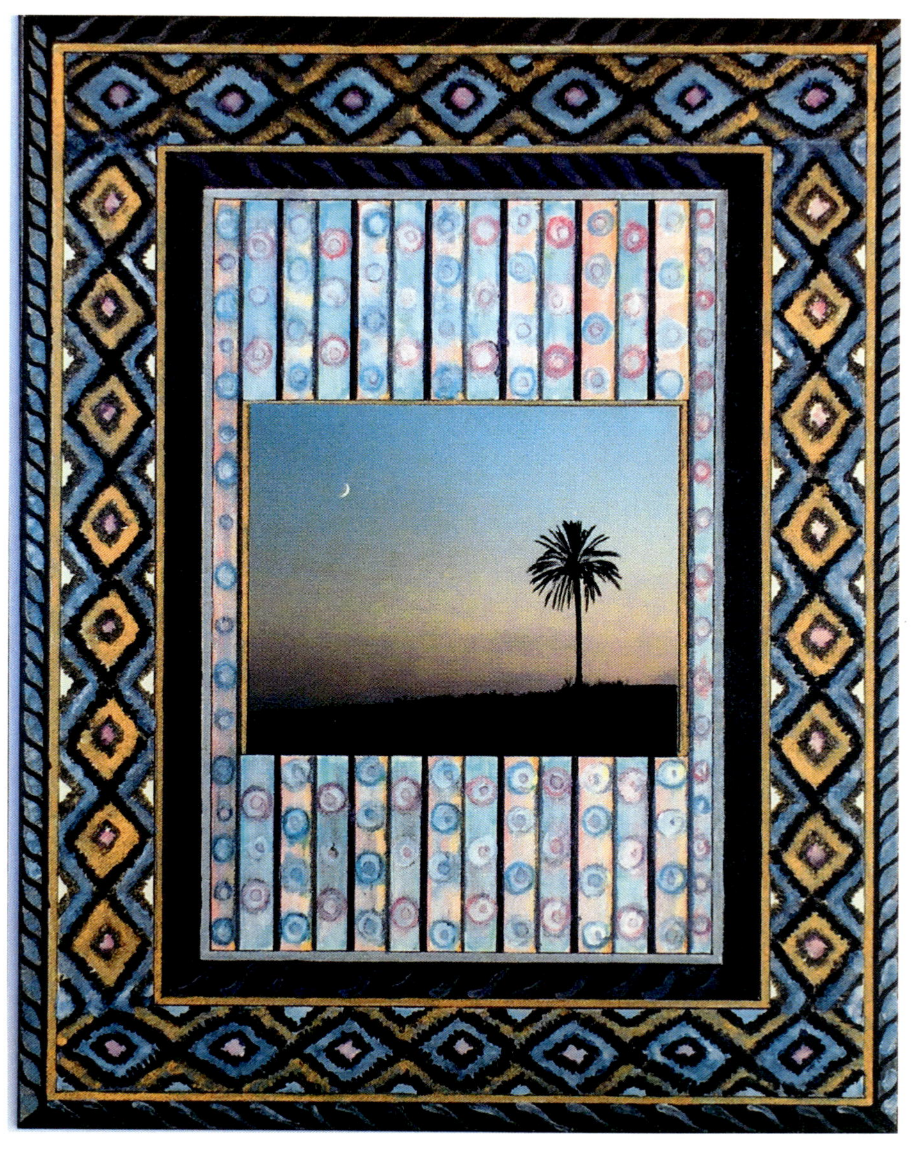

"Arabesques" greeting card set (1995) original size 6 ½ x 4 ¾

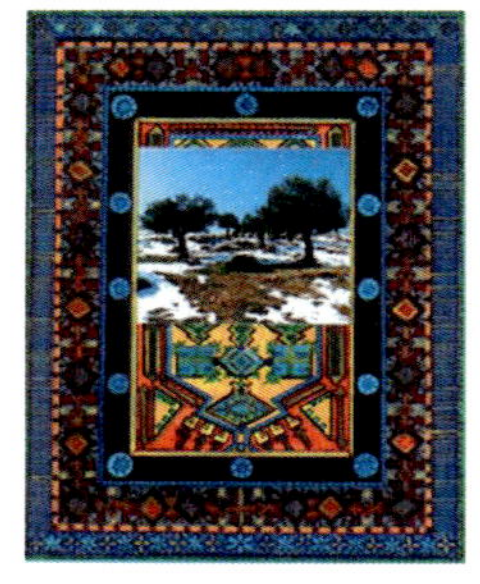 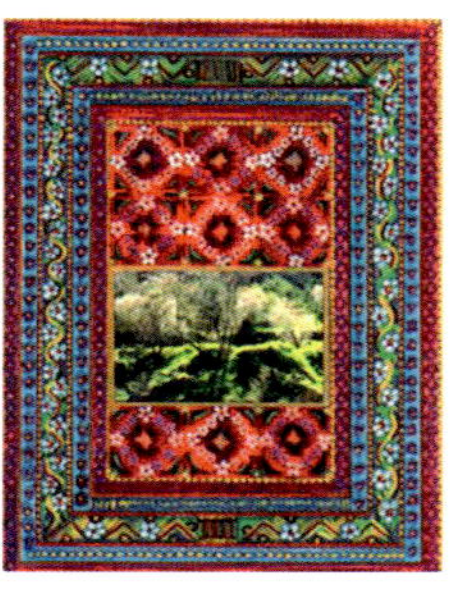 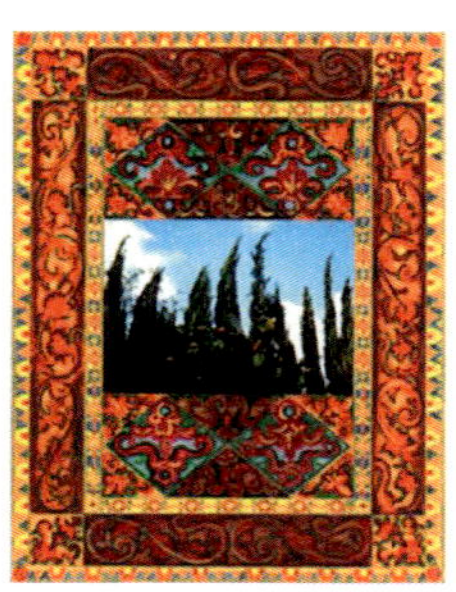 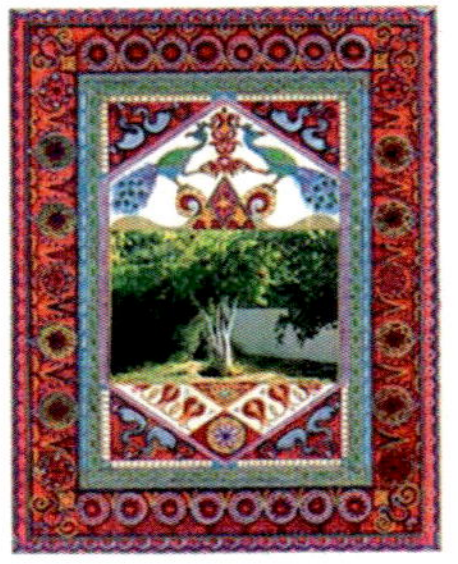 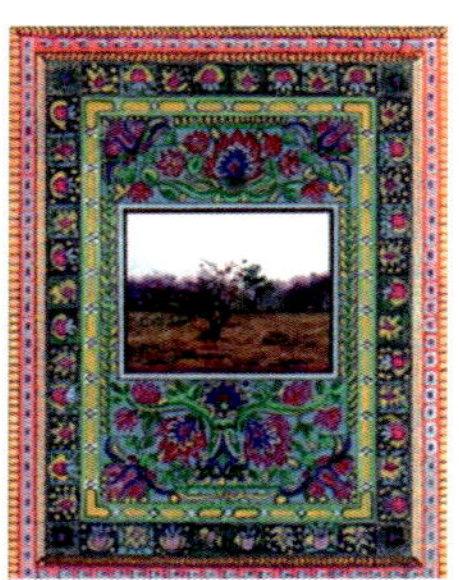

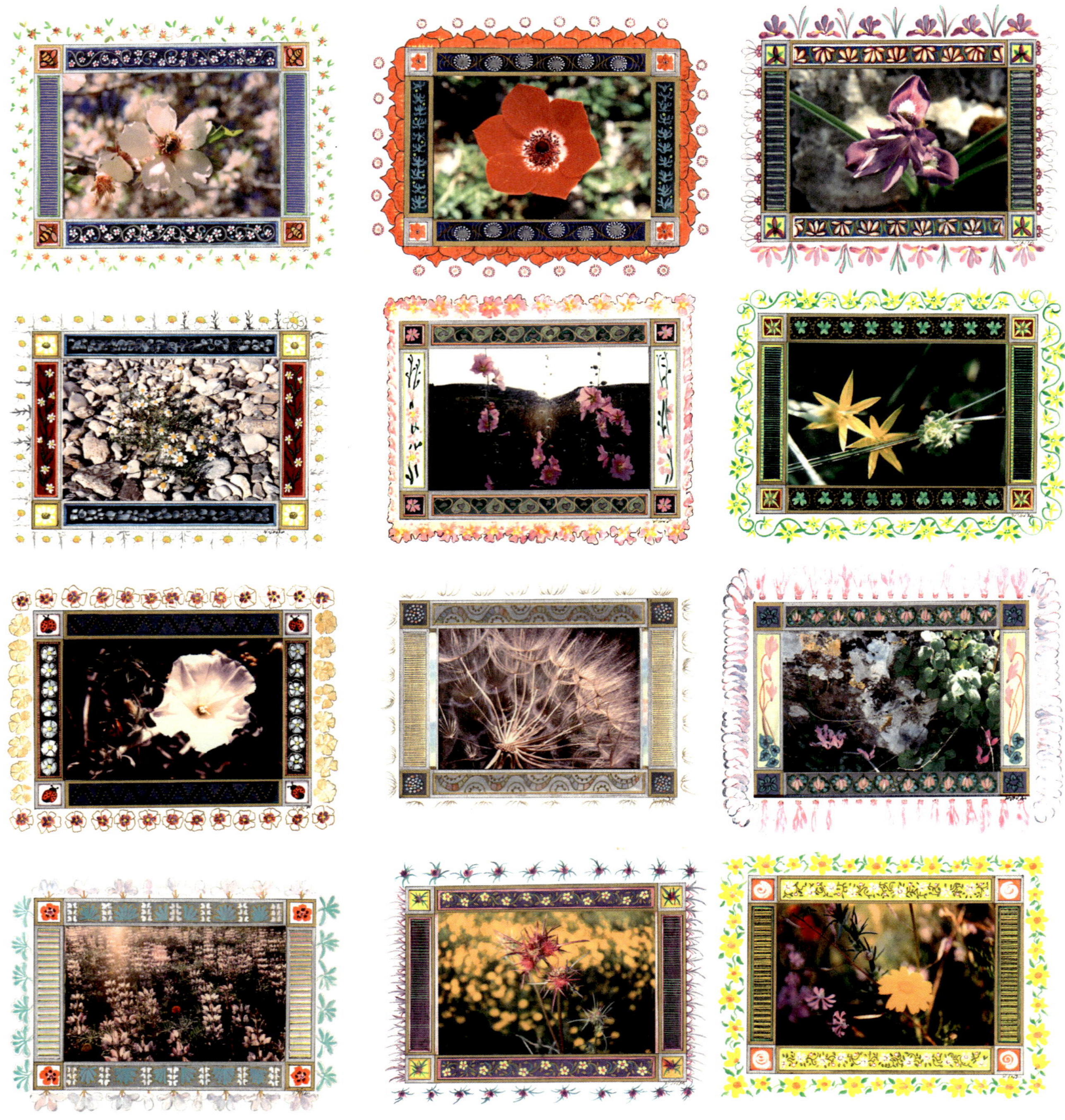

Wildflowers of Israel (1991)

Left to right – Top row: Almond; Anemone; Iris; Second row: Chamomile; Hollyhock; Gold Crocus; Third row: Morning Glory; Dry Goatsbeard; Cyclamen; Fourth row: Lupin; Syrian Thistle; Daisy

These designs, photographs with painted borders, were published between 1990 and 1998 as greeting card sets. These are a small sampling of native wildflowers in Israel.

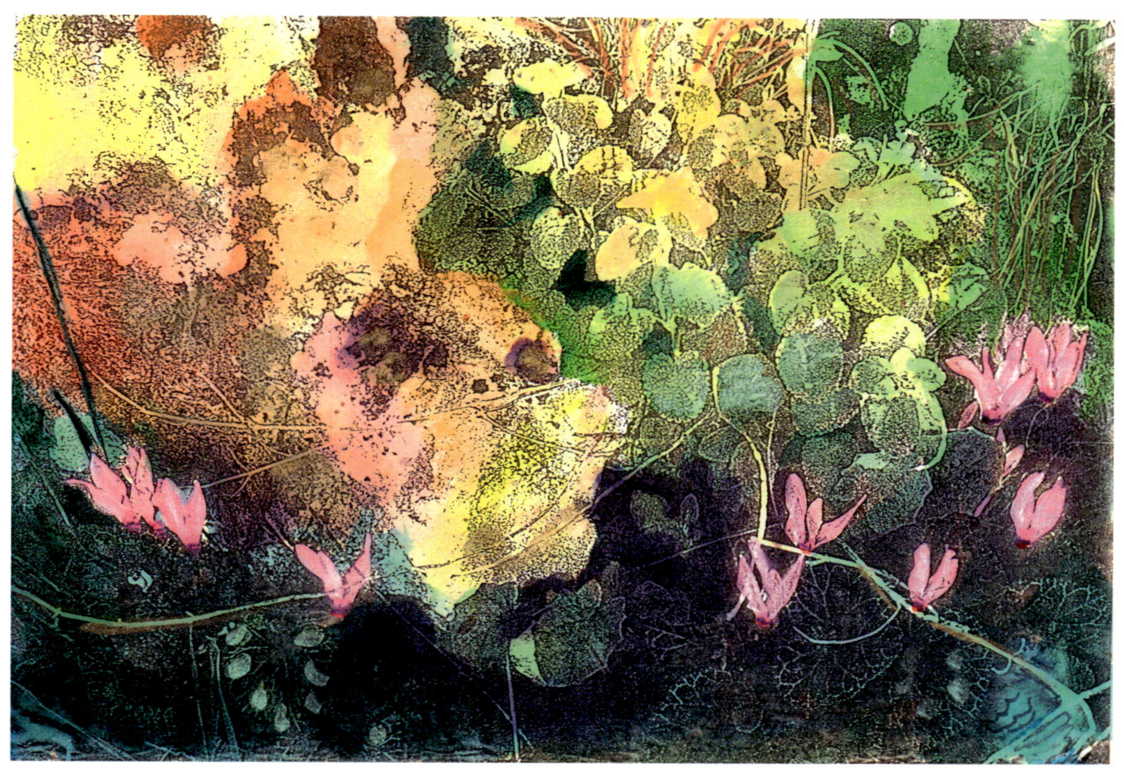

Cyclamen (1993) mixed-media on rice paper, 10 x 13 in.

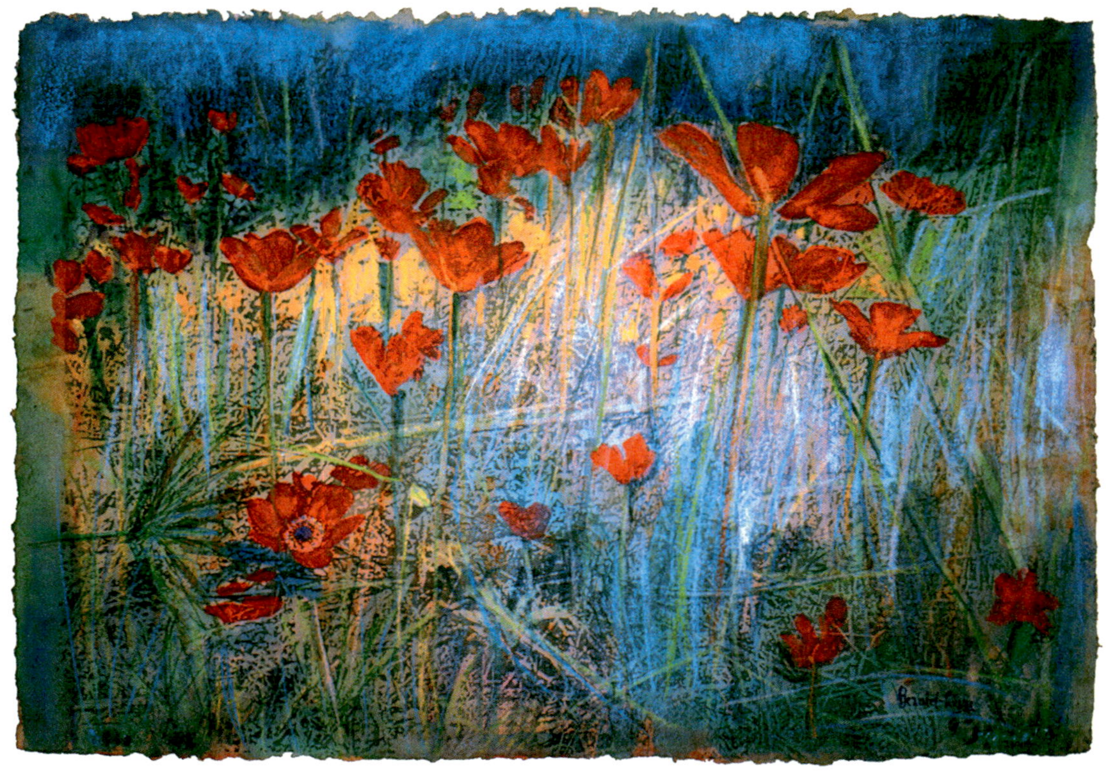

Anenomes (1993) mixed-media on handmade paper, 16 x 20 in.

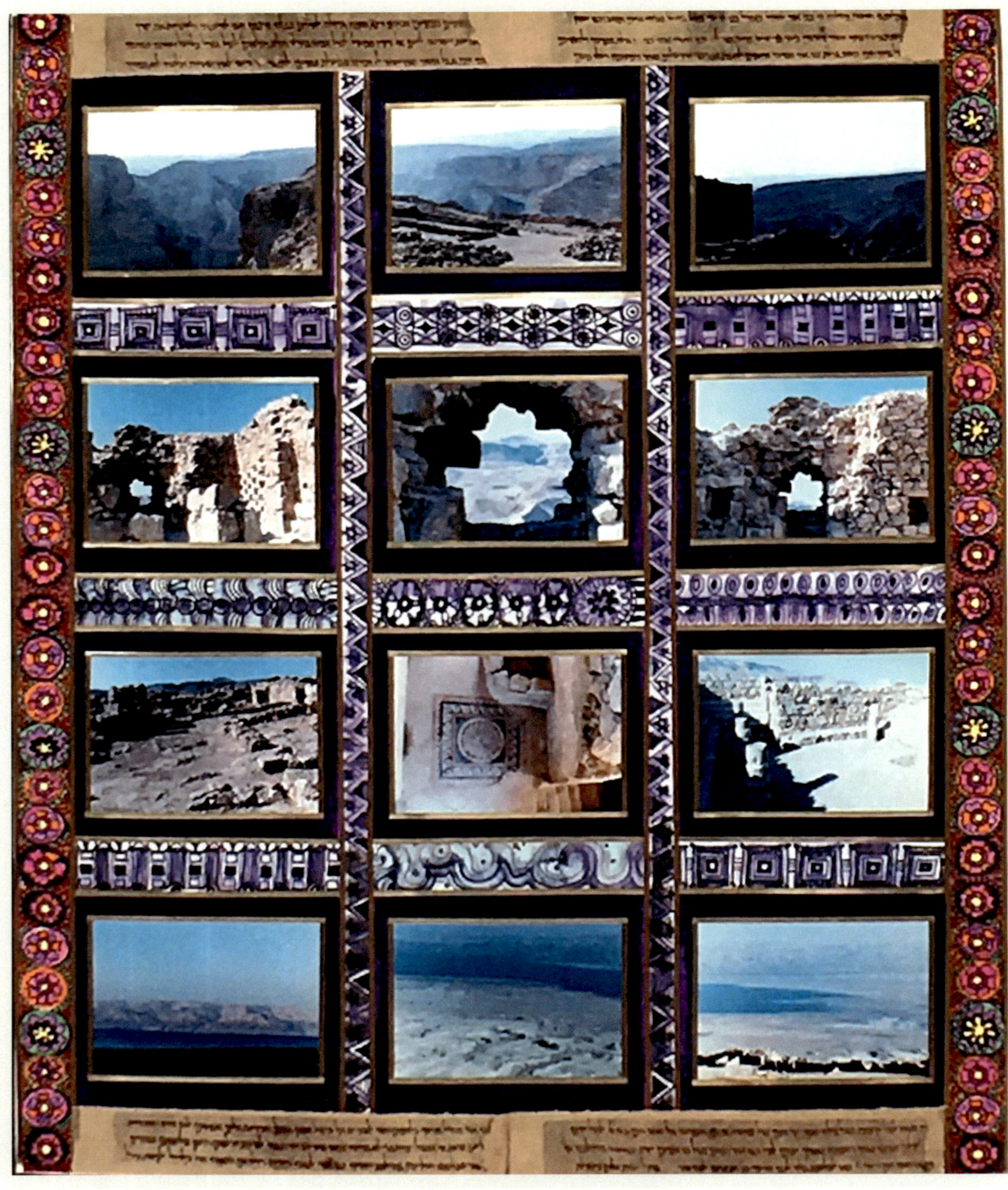

Masada (37 x 30 in.)

Containing the remains of a fortress and a palace, Masada sits atop an isolated plateau on the edge of the Judean desert overlooking the Dead Sea. After the First Jewish-Roman War, in 72 C.E., a siege of the fortress by troops of the Roman Empire led to the mass suicide of Jewish rebels rather than facing surrender to the Roman troops. The text at the top and bottom of the panel is a facsimile of the Dead Sea Scrolls, specifically a passage from the scroll "The War of the Sons of Light and the Sons of Darkness."

We received a commission from the management of the Masada site to produce a poster from the design on the opposite page. For the first time, we decided to include a dedication, so, in the bottom right corner of the poster, in 10 point letters, we printed, "Dedicated to Saul Spilke," Chaim's father. We had visited Masada with Chaim's parents when the photographs on the poster were taken.

Saul had immigrated to America from Poland in 1933. His original name was Bezalel, but, like so many names, it was changed, so I only time his original name was used was on Chaim's bar mitzvah when his father was called to the Torah. Saul was aware, even proud of the fact, that Bezalel was the artist and architect who was in charge of fashioning the Tabernacle in the wilderness and all of its vessels and accouterments. With his father's permission, Chaim had taken his father's birth name as his family name in Israel.

Soon after the poster was released, we were contacted by the rabbi from the synagogue in Chaim's hometown. He had purchased the poster, read the dedication, and upon his return he visited Saul and gave him the poster. It was a special delivery. Saul died that week.

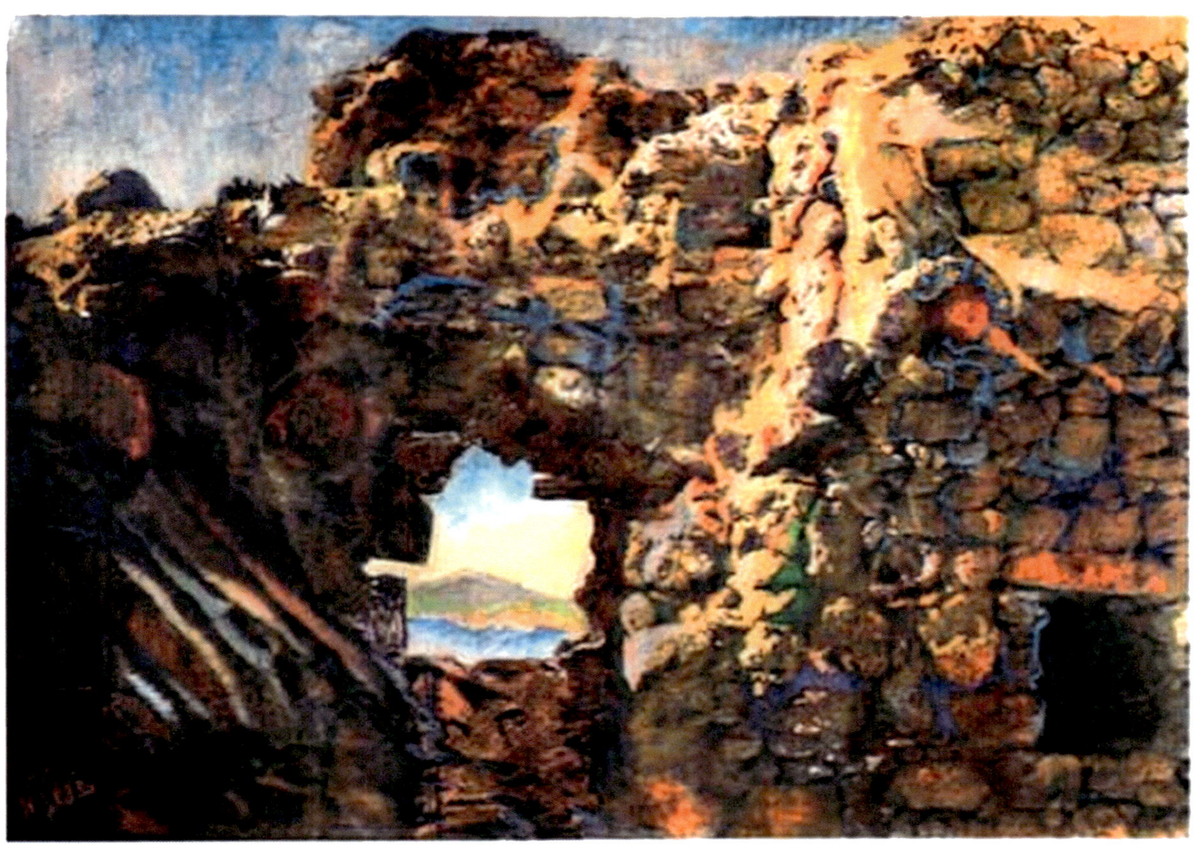

Masada (1994) mixed-media on rice paper, 29 x 37 in.

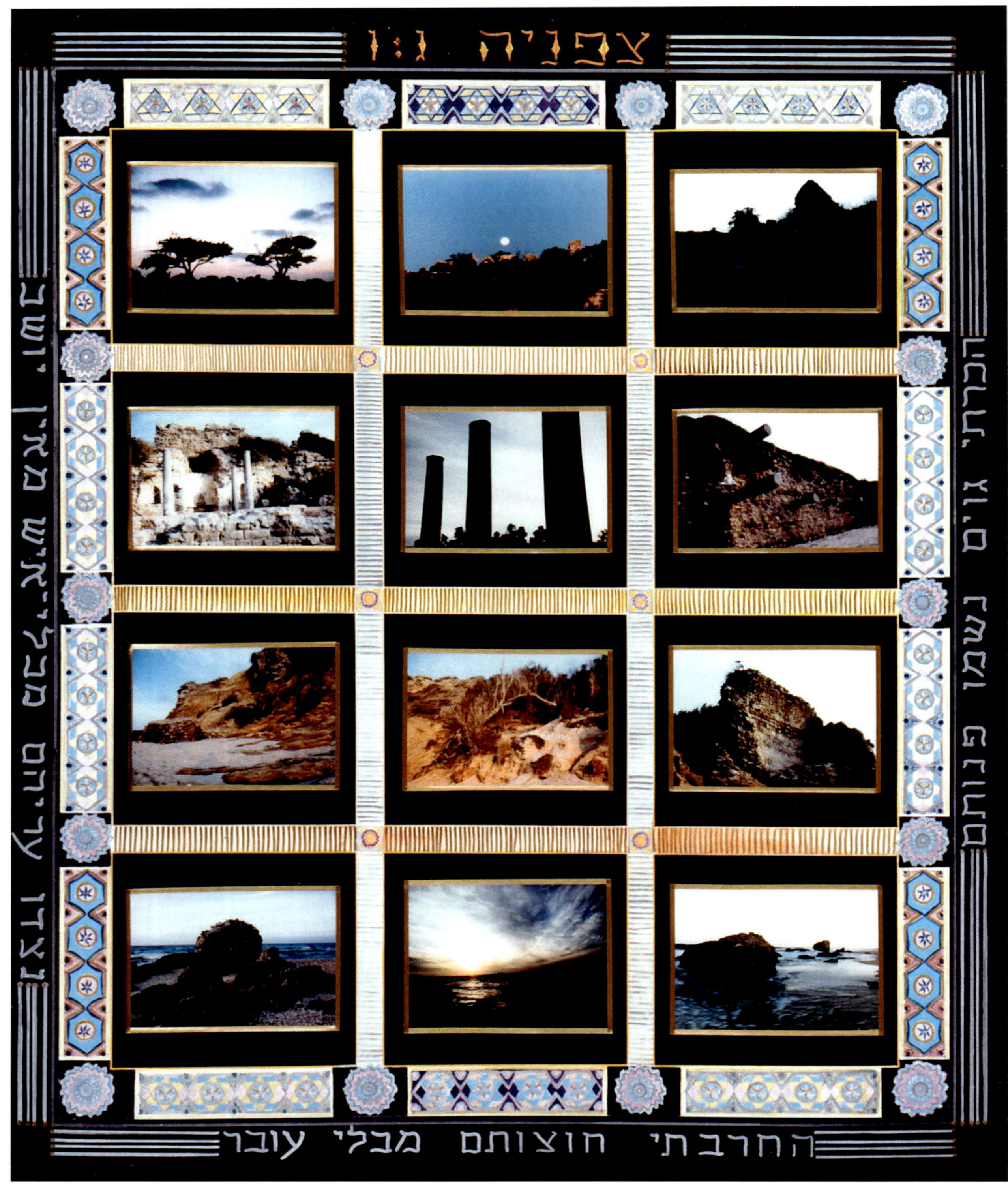

Ruins of Ashkelon I (37 x 30 in.)

"I have cut off the nations: their towers are desolate; I made their streets waste, that none passeth by: their cities are destroyed, so that there is no man, that there is none inhabitant. " - Zephaniah 3:6.

One of the oldest inhabited cities in the world, Ashkelon was conquered by the Egyptians, the Canaanites, the Philistines, the Assyrians, the Babylonians, the Greeks, the Phoenicians, the Hasmoneans, the Romans, the Persians, the Arabs, the Crusaders, the Mamluks, the Ottoman Turks, and the British before it fell to Israeli forces in 1948.

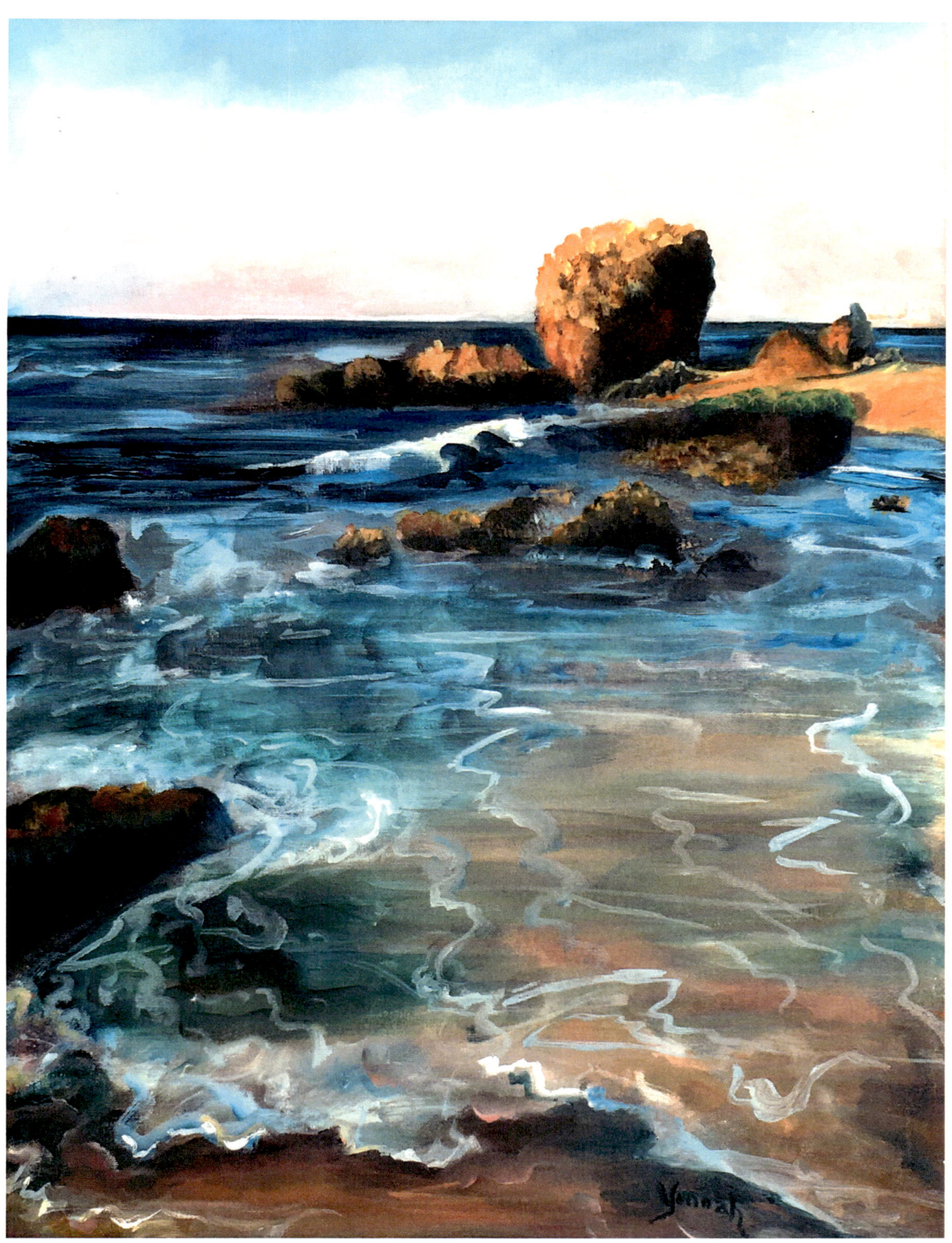

Ancient Harbor (2017) *Yonnah Ben Levy,* acrylics on canvas, 23 x 18 in.

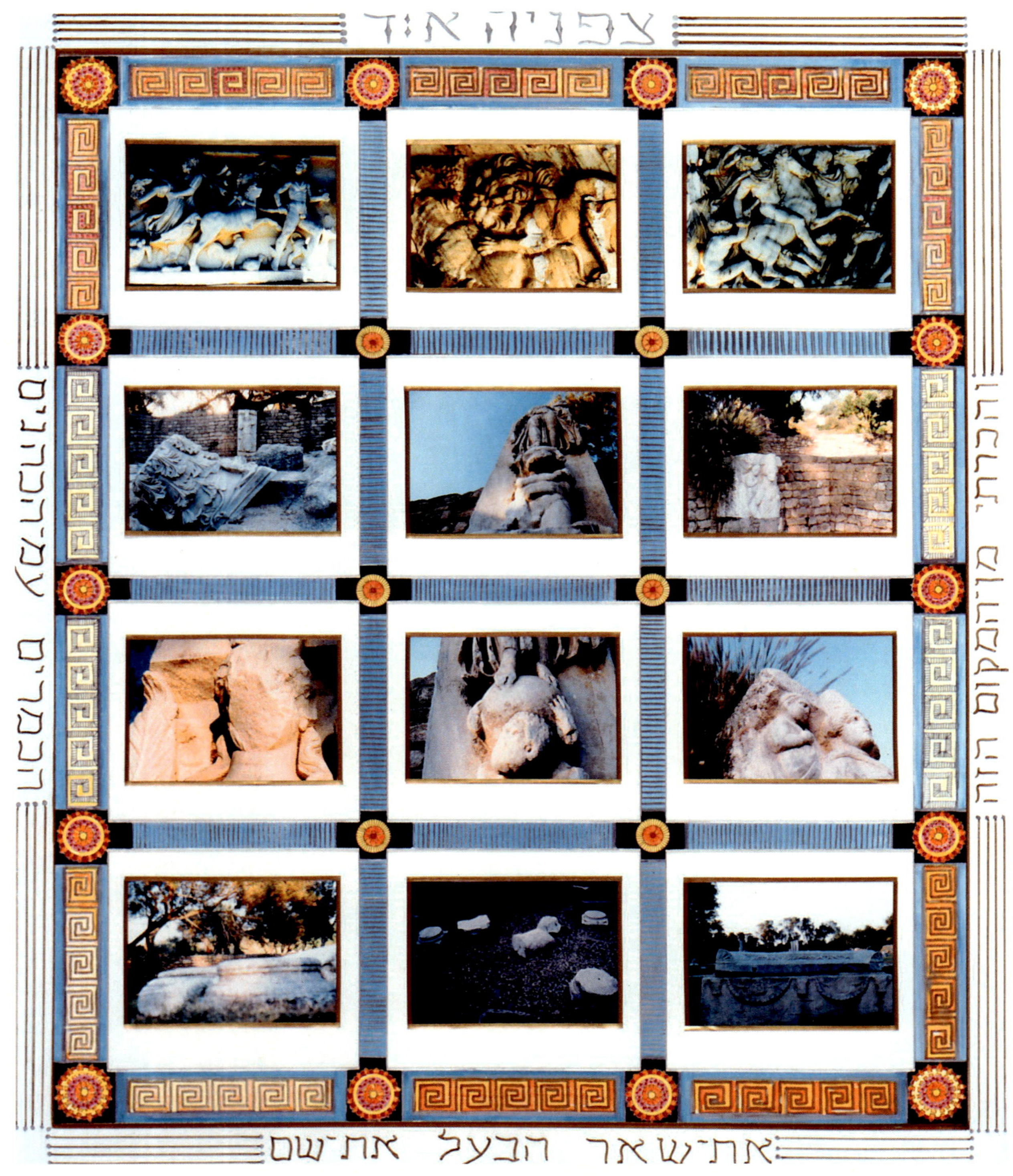

Ruins of Ashkelon II (37 x 30 in.)

"I will also stretch out mine hand upon Judah, and upon all the inhabitants of Jerusalem; and I will cut off the remnant of Baal from this place, and the name of the idolatrous priests with the priests."
- Zephaniah 1:4

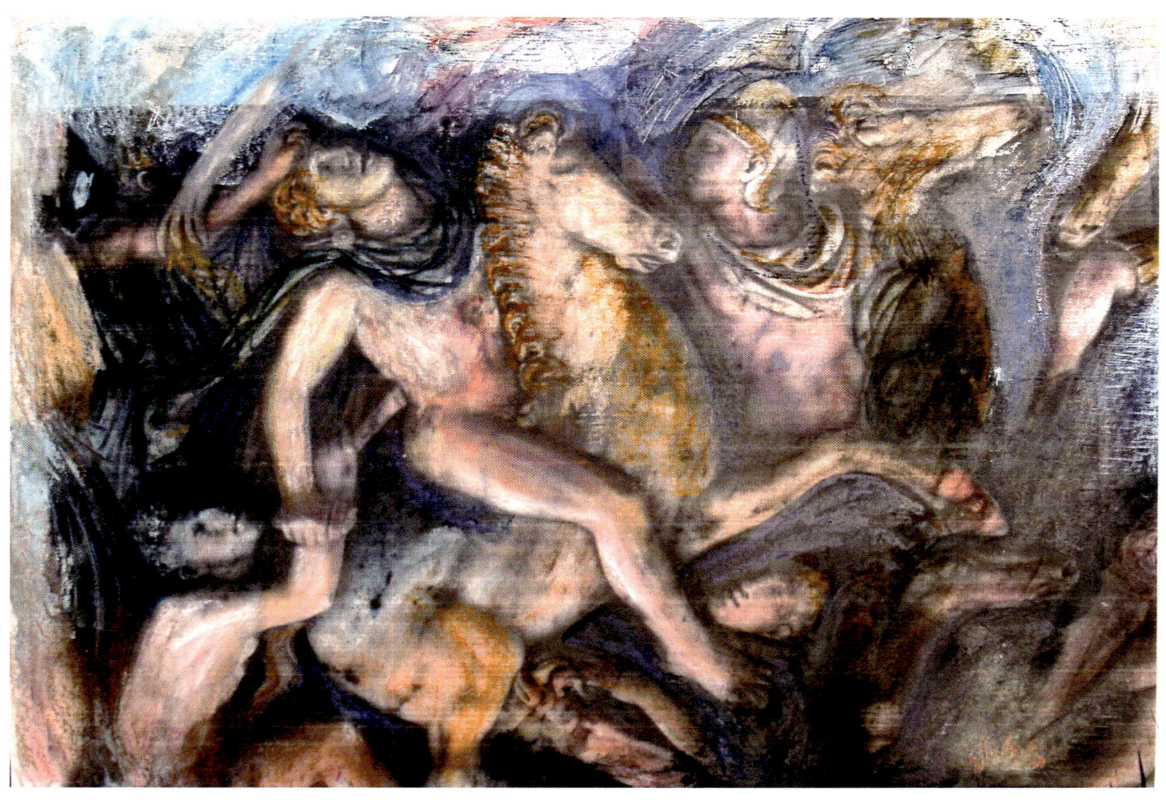

Roman Sarcophagus (1992) mixed-media with photography and oil pastels, 28 x 40 in.

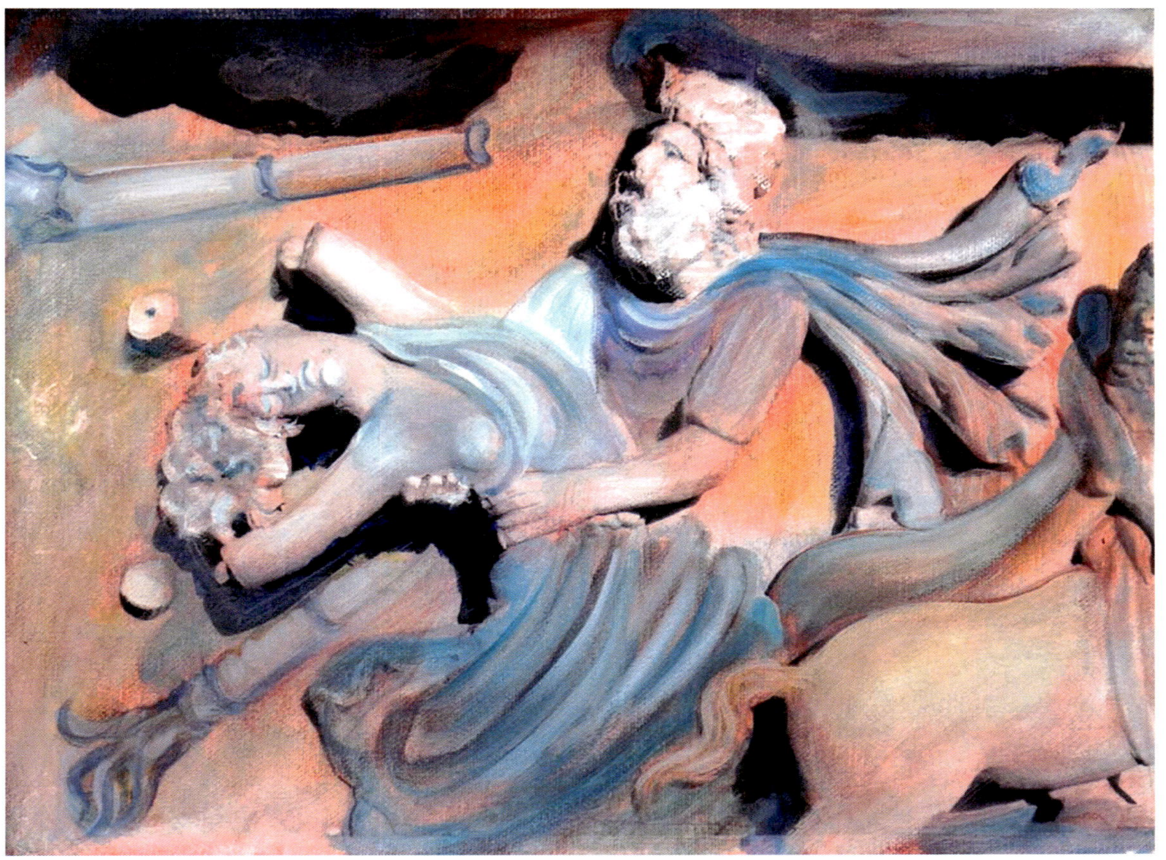

Abduction of Persephone (2014) mixed-media with acrylics on canvas, 8 x 11 in.

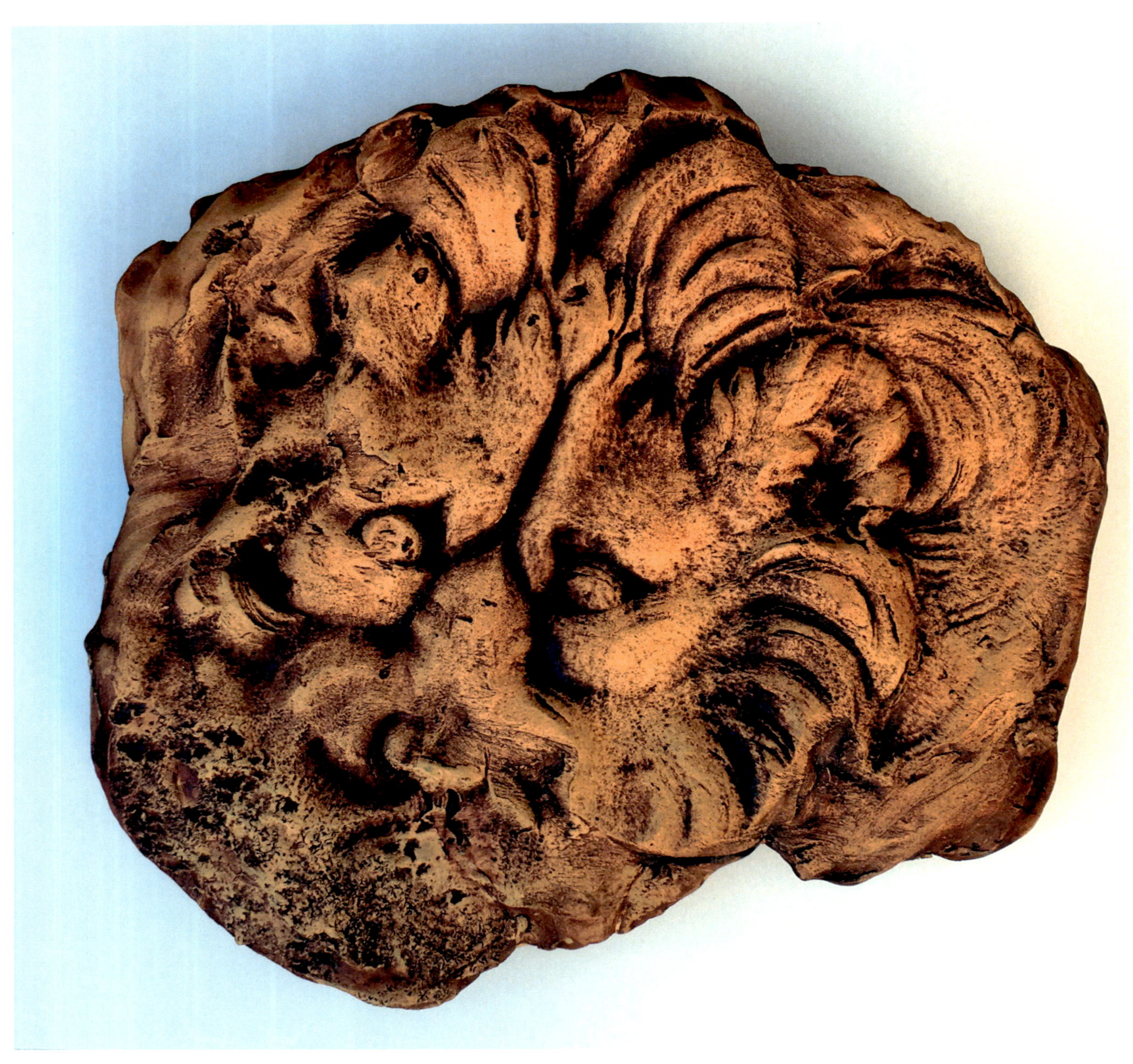

Lion (2017) *Chaim Bezalel*, wall mounted high fired ceramic tile, 12 x 12 in.

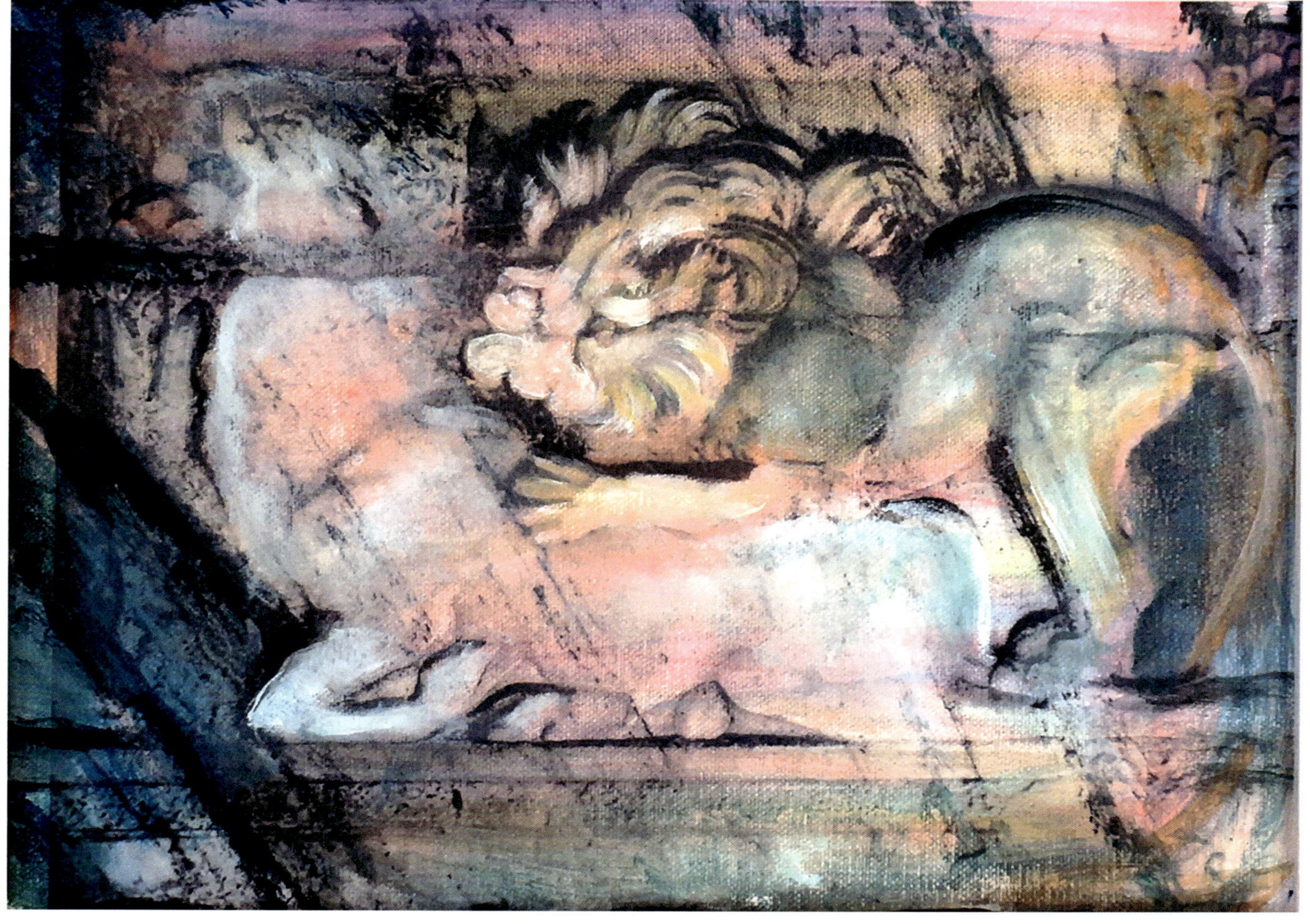

Lion Goring a Bull (2014) mixed-media with acrylics on canvas, 8 x 11 in.

This tableau is from the Roman sarcophagus that is located a short walk from our home in Ashkelon. Whatever symbolism, if any, was intended by the original artist who carved it into marble, symbols can have a wider currency. Especially if the symbolic forms are animals.

The former section of this book, "Bowls of Blessing," quoted the oracles attributed to either Jacob or Moses over the twelve sons who became the twelve tribes. It is well known that the symbol of Judah is the lion, from Jacob's blessing. It is not as well known that the symbol of the tribe of Joseph is the bullock or the ox or the unicorn or the oryx (an Arabian antelope) depending upon the translation of Moses' blessing.

"His firstling bullock, majesty is his; and his horns are the horns of the wild-ox; with them he shall gore the peoples all of them, even the ends of the earth" - Deuteronomy 33:17

In some translations he shall merely push them instead of goring them. In this instance, it looks like the bull is the one being gored. For sixty years after the northern tribes of Israel seceded from the united kingdom under the sovereignty of Judah, there was constant war between them. This was followed by an alliance cemented by a political marriage. This was followed by a coup d'état in the northern kingdom of Samaria involving a double regicide followed in Judah by a bloody coup by Athaliah, the queen mother, involving her murder of all but one possible claimants to the throne. Not long afterwards, exile and captivity followed, accompanied by serial conquests of the land of Israel, including by the Romans.

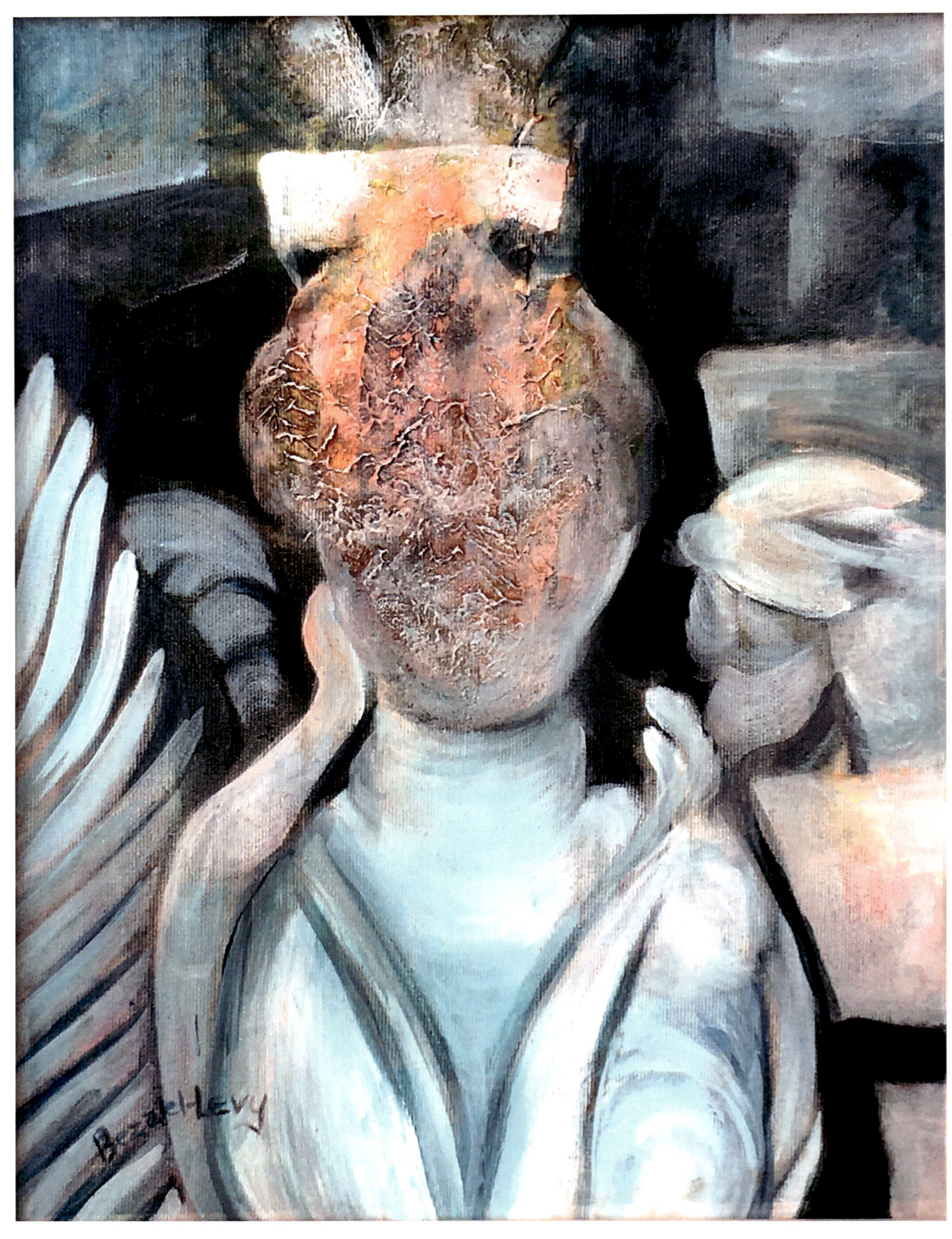

Effaced Nike (2015) acrylics on canvas, 16 x 12 in.

46

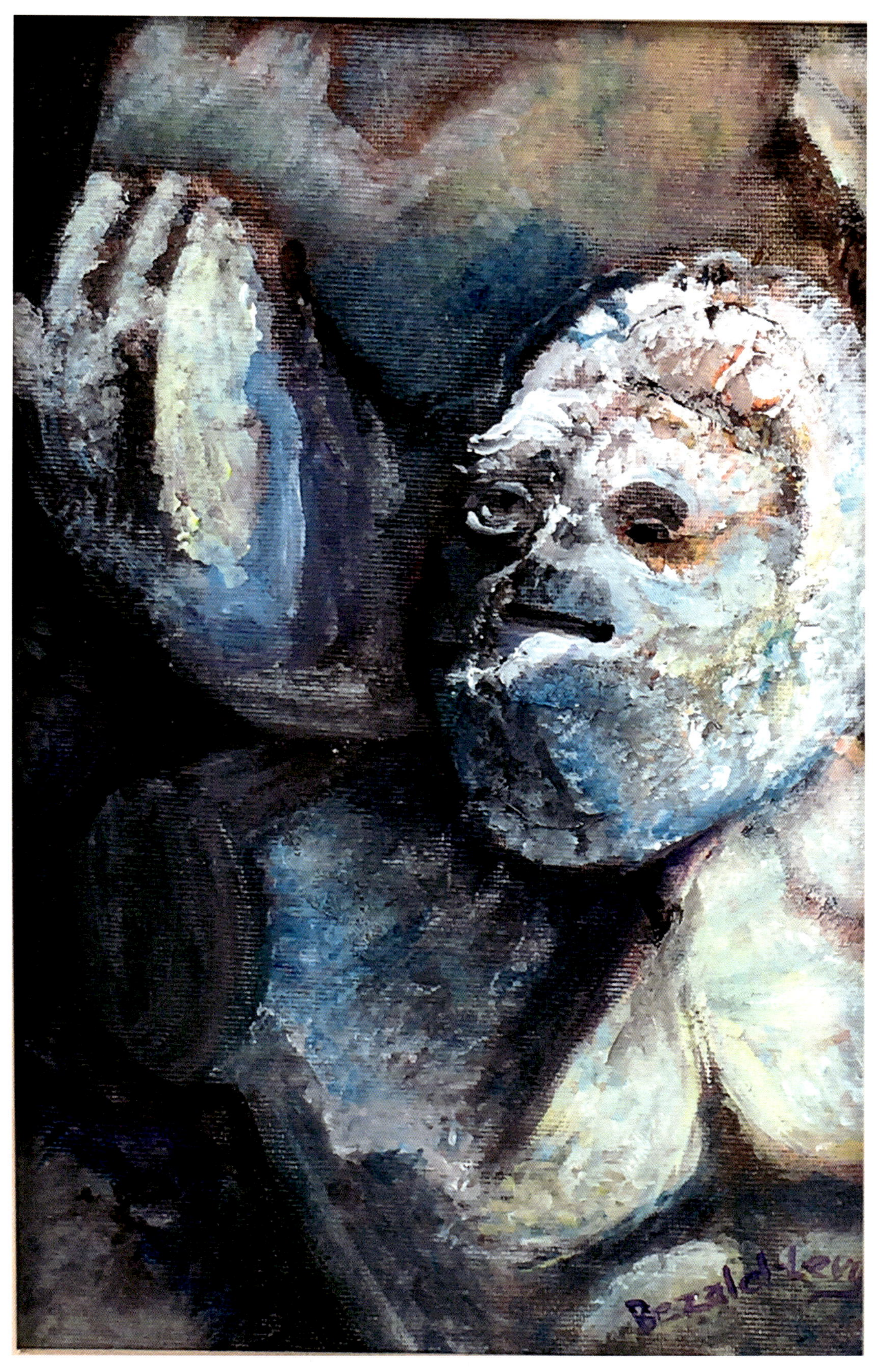

Armless Atlas (2015) acrylics on canvas, 11 x 7 in.

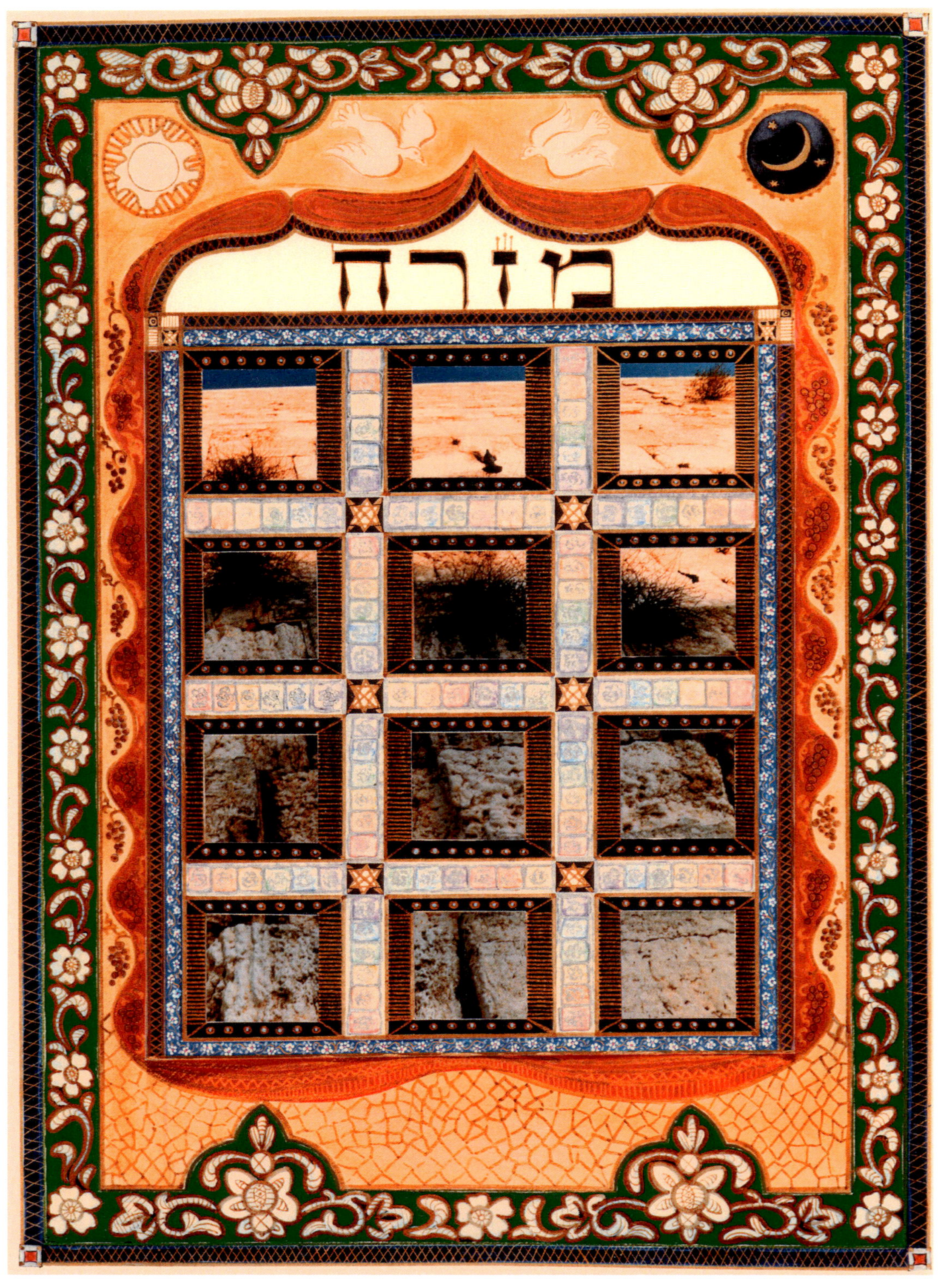

Mizrach (29 x 20 in.)

Mizrach means East in Hebrew. Traditionally hung on the eastern wall of a synagogue or sometimes in a home, it reminds those who pray to face Jerusalem, as Solomon prayed in his dedication of the Temple (1Kings 8:22-52). The twelve photographs are sections of a single photograph of the stones of the Western Wall cut into twelve squares.

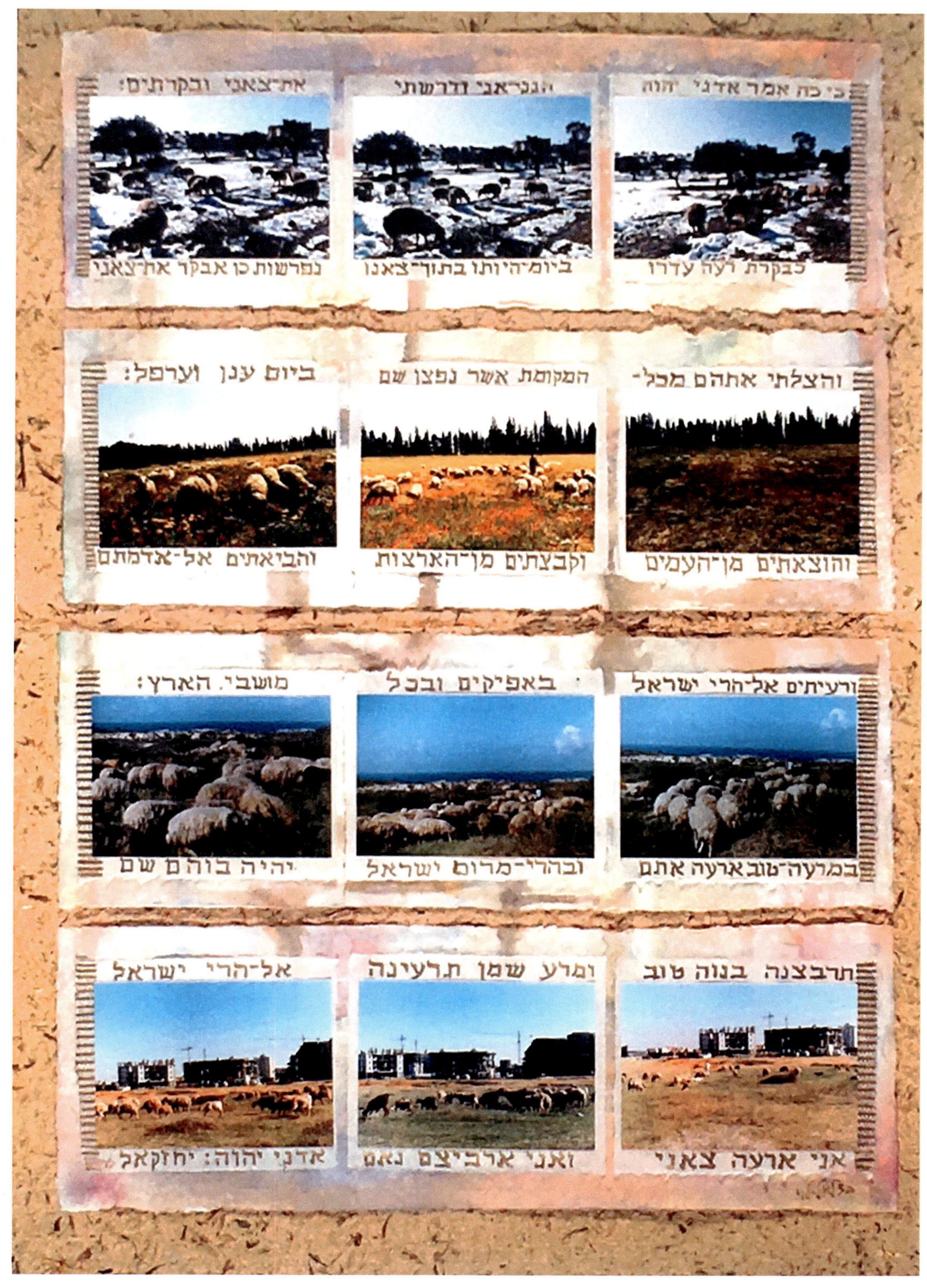

Sheep (40 x 28 in.)

"For thus saith the Lord God; Behold, I, even I, will both search my sheep, and seek them out. As a shepherd seeketh out his flock in the day that he is among his sheep that are scattered; so will I seek out my sheep, and will deliver them out of all places where they have been scattered in the cloudy and dark day... " - Ezekiel 34

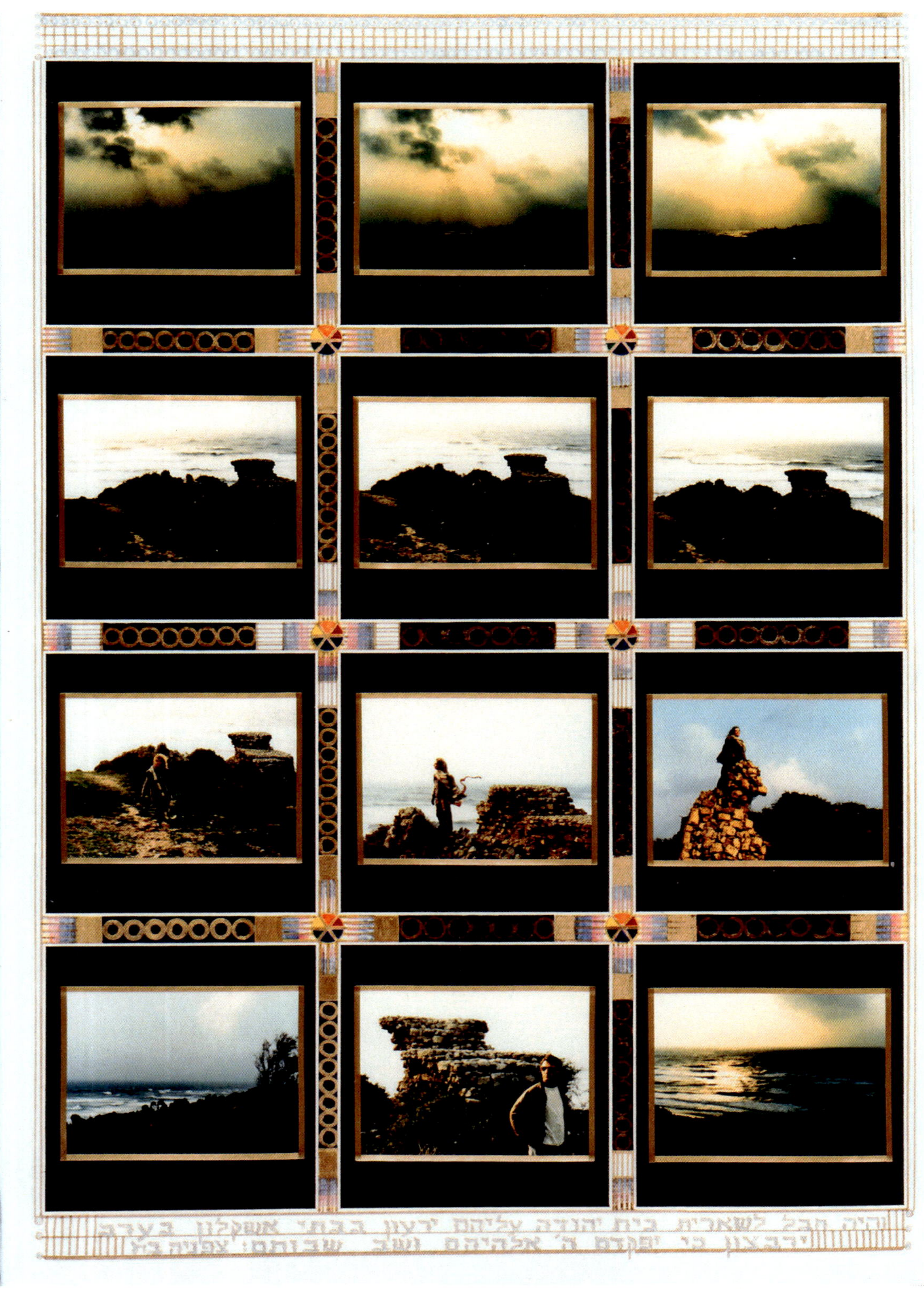

After the Storm (40 x 28 in.)

"And the coast shall be for the remnant of the house of Judah; they shall feed thereupon: in the houses of Ashkelon shall they lie down in the evening: for the LORD their God shall visit them, and turn away their captivity." - Zephaniah 2:7

The panel on the opposite page shows Chaim and Yonnah on the walls of Ashkelon. It was the last of the series. The photographs in the panel were taken on February 28, 1991, the day the Gulf War ended, which happened to fall on the holiday of Purim. Chaim had been drafted into the Israeli army at age 40 at the start of the Gulf War in January. He was released from basic training on the day that the war ended, the day the Scud missiles stopped falling on Israel. Purim is all about the reversal of fortunes, in fact the word means "lots."

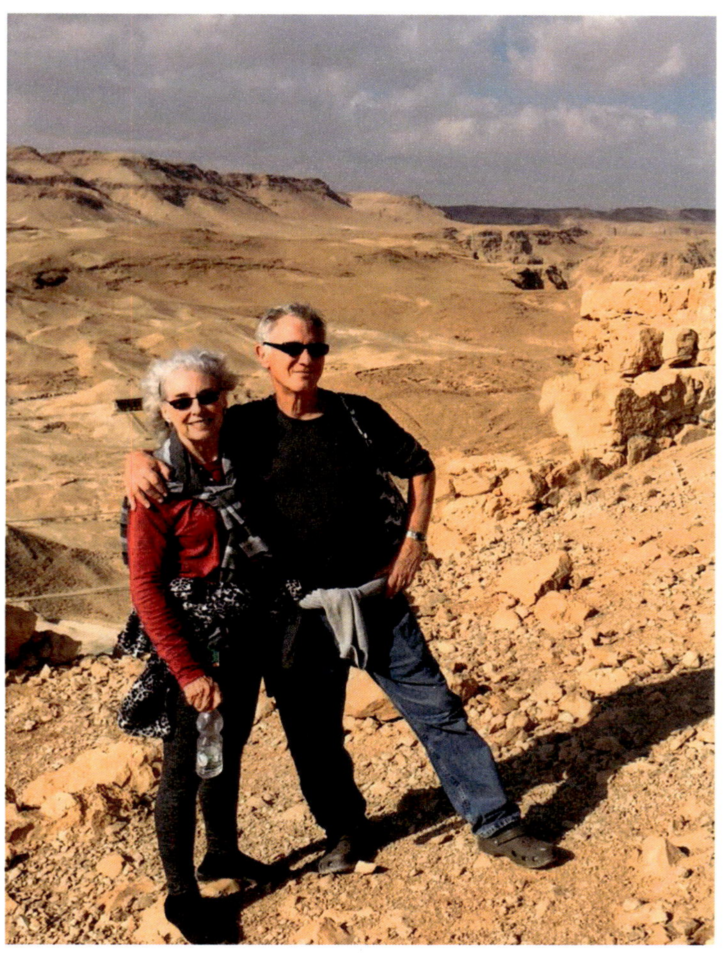

Yonnah Ben Levy and Chaim Bezalel met in Jerusalem in 1988. They are dual citizens of Israel and the United States. Yonnah was raised in Seattle, Washington. She is a lifelong artist and teacher having received her Masters of Art for Teachers at University of Washington. She also studied ceramics at the Corcoran Gallery in Washington D. C. with Teruo Hara, a renowned master potter. Chaim Bezalel studied film at Northwestern University and work in mixed-media including photography, painting, ceramics, writing, and music. Chaim and Yonnah collaborate under their combined signature, Bezalel-Levy. Many of their paintings have been commissioned or purchased for public venues and they have exhibited in several countries. An upcoming exhibition, including some of the works in this book, will be held at the Cambridge Museum of Classical Archaeology in England in 2019.

More from Dekel Press
info and orders at *www.dekelpress.com*

east and west   *near and far*

Dekel Press

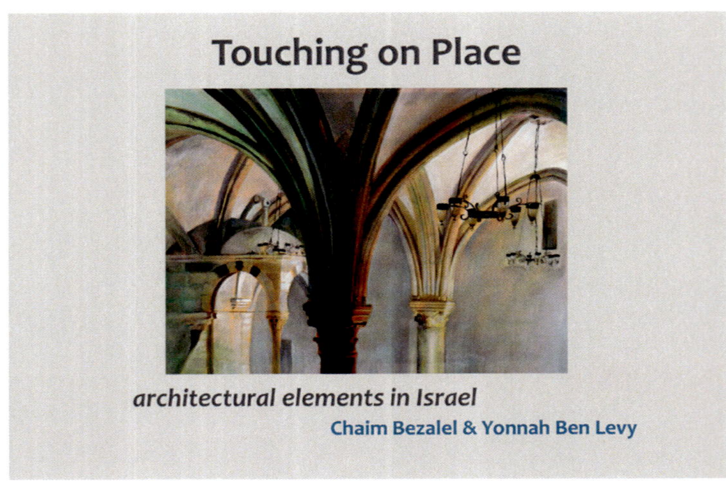

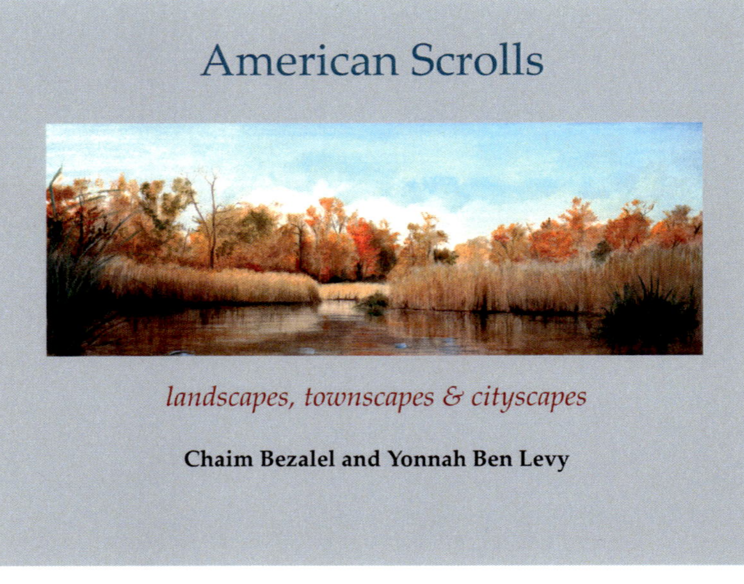

ISBN 978-0-9995958-0-0, paperback, 90 p. 6" x 9"

Seventy-seven original paintings done over twenty-five years convey the history of the past two millennia in this historic land. The book is arranged geographically with an explanation of each region and site. $20

ISBN 978-0-9995958-4-8, paperback, 134 p. 8 1/2" x 11"

150 mostly panoramic paintings from different parts of America including Autumn Scrolls, Pacific Scrolls, Gulf Scrolls, Desert Scrolls, and Community. Many of these paintings are now in public collections. $30

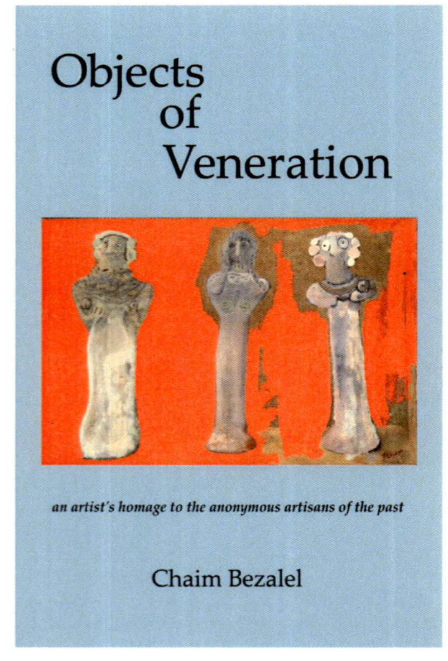

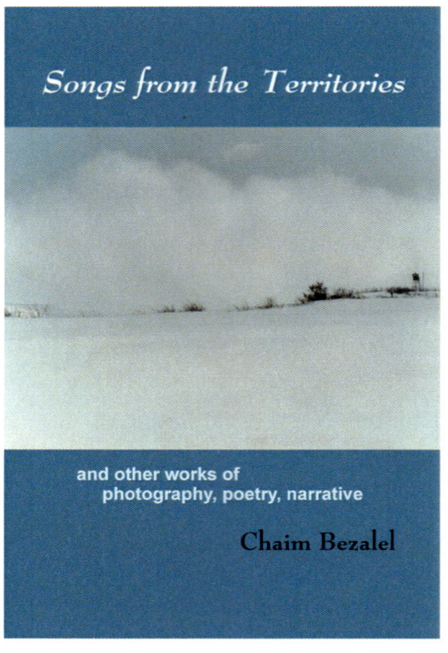

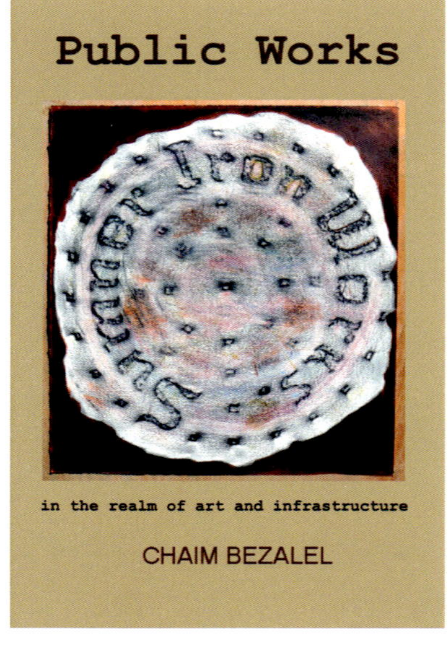

ISBN 978-0-9995958-1-7, 90 p. 9" x 6"

ISBN 978-0-9995958-5-5, 120 p. 9" x 6"

ISBN 978-0-9995958-2-4,120 p. 9" X 6"

Paintings and sculpture inspired by devotional objects from around the world in the artist's or in other private and public collections. Includes a 33 page essay, "The Talmud, a Brief Travelogue." $20

In 1988, a 38 year old ex-hippie, ex-stockbroker on the lam boards a plane to Israel, where he has never been, with a one way ticket and two suitcases. Two years later, during the Gulf War, he is drafted into the Israeli army reserves. This is his journal. $15

A cross-genre exploration of the meaning of community and the place of art through poems, song lyrics, art, photography, and 6 essays. on art including Between Decadence and Renaissance; Why You Hate Art (You know you do); and the Evolution of Propaganda. $20